BROKEN

YET DESTINED TO BE HEALED

BROKEN

YET DESTINED TO BE HEALED

ORLANDO C. ROWE

BROKEN, YET DESTINED TO BE HEALED
Copyright © 2023 by Orlando C. Rowe

ISBN: 978-1-4866-2453-9
eBook ISBN: 978-1-4866-2454-6

Word Alive Press
119 De Baets Street Winnipeg, MB R2J 3R9
www.wordalivepress.ca

WORD ALIVE
—PRESS—

Cataloguing in Publication information can be obtained from Library and Archives Canada.

DEDICATION

TO MY MOTHER, Mrs. Sonia Rowe. You have been a source of strength and encouragement. Mommy, I love and appreciate you.

To my grandmother, Fay Beckford. Words cannot express how grateful I am for the blessing you have been in my life.

To my siblings: Jermaine, Donya, Sherone, Leo. You have all been a great blessing and pillars of strength.

To all the broken and the disenfranchised people around the world who will read this book. May God lift you up when you fall.

CONTENTS

ACKNOWLEDGEMENTS

THROUGH THE YEARS, many people have been a motivating factor toward the completion of this book. I want to take some time to acknowledge these marvellous people of God.

I want to first thank You, Lord, for the strength and endurance You have given me to complete this work of Yours. May You use this work to bless many others.

I want to also thank you, Mommy Sonia. There was a time when you used to call me every day just to ask if I was ok. Mommy, you are the best, and I love you.

To my siblings—Jermaine, Donya, Sherone, and Leo. Without you guys, life wouldn't be the same for me. I love and appreciate you.

To Daddy. We miss you dearly. You still live in our hearts each day.

PREFACE

I HAVE SEEN a prevalent condition all around us, from the lonely streets to the most occupied and esteemed places on earth. This condition I call brokenness. I am often touched by the pain of others, and when I myself am wounded, I tend to want to make a difference. *Broken, yet Destined to Be Healed* is not only inspired by the need I see around me but mostly by the need I have experienced within. It seeks to promote healing as a right for the broken. Healing is not only possible but necessary for us to live the life God created us to live. My hope is that even though we must all travel through some sort of brokenness, we will address it from a place of faith, knowing that from the ashes of our brokenness, God wants to make our lives more beautiful.

For many years I struggled with a wounded spirit. Some wounds can be seen with the naked eye and addressed by physical means, but who can help a broken spirit? In his sermon "The Cause and Cure of a Wounded Spirit," Charles Spurgeon comments: "Every man sooner or later will have some kind of infirmity to bear."[1] This I find to be very true. I have had the privilege of working and interacting with people from different walks of life, and one thing I find in common among us is brokenness. Each person will have to bear their fair share of brokenness.

I have also found that brokenness can be beautiful. Depending on how we view it, our brokenness can be the most rewarding thing that can ever happen to us, because brokenness often releases our hidden potential. As the purity of gold is realized in a furnace, so too is our potential released through the crevices of our brokenness. Imagine if the goldsmith never hammered his gold and brought it into warm temperatures. Now compare fine gold with that which is unrefined and you will begin to understand why I say that a broken place, where fire can be most prevalent, can be the most beautiful place.

The artwork on the cover of this book is inspired by the Japanese art of repairing broken pottery with gold. In this process, the repaired object becomes more beautiful than it was before. I truly believe that as we walk with God, He endeavours to do the same with us, to make our lives much more beautiful and valuable than they were before. We must understand that God knows what He is about.

As you read through the pages of this book, be encouraged. The enormity of your brokenness doesn't matter; what matters is the magnitude of God's love. God loves us so much that He

---

[1] "The Cause and Cure of a Wounded Spirit," The Spurgeon Center, accessed August 12, 2023, https://www.spurgeon.org/resource-library/sermons/the-cause-and-cure-of-a-wounded-spirit/#flipbook/.

eagerly wants to heal us. There is no brokenness that God can't make more beautiful. There is also no valley too deep for God to guide you through. My hope is that this book will help you to address your brokenness by faith. I pray that your brokenness will make you more beautiful.

INTRODUCTION

SOMETIMES BROKENNESS CAN be the most wonderful thing. I speak of brokenness as a battered and utterly defeated state, yet a state in which the most precious life lessons can be learnt. What seems like chaos might be the most precise piecing together of our lives. Often when we look back in hindsight, we realize that God was working out His miracle all along.

Broken, yet Destined to be Healed conveys the raw deal of a broken person. Brokenness can make us vulnerable to the forces that fight against us, yet it can also put us in the most fluid of positions to be changed. Consider the sovereign hands of God as He molds us like a potter does clay. Molding can seem like brokenness, yet it's nothing more than God forming us into His masterpieces. God knows what He is about.

Brokenness is a worldwide problem. It happens to everyone, regardless of our race, education, or experience. It happens to the sinner and the saint, the humble and the proud. Regardless of our expertise, there are areas of our lives in which we fall apart, so this book was written for everyone, everywhere, and at any age.

Christ was so broken when He cried, *"My God, my God, why have you forsaken Me?"* (Matthew 27:46). Consider that Jesus was the perfect man, with a perfect heart and a perfect understanding, yet He was being critically broken. In the flesh, Jesus was being torn into pieces, yet in the Spirit, He was being glorified. Imagine that Jesus could have stopped all of this yet chose the will of God over the brokenness He was experiencing—over and over. Jesus told His disciples that He had to complete His Father's work (Luke 2:49). He didn't allow the process to overthrow Him, but rather He looked to the purpose of His brokenness, which was salvation for us all.

Throughout the years, I've had my own share of brokenness. Once I was so broken that I utterly wanted to die, and I begged God to take my life, yet nothing could have snatched me out of His sovereign hands. During that time, I discovered that brokenness can catapult us further into God's divine plan. The Bible says that sorrow is better than laughter, because sorrow makes the heart better (Ecclesiastes 7:3). Imagine the great importance of our own brokenness! Even the little birds discover that from broken branches, they can build a beautiful home. How much more can we use the brokenness we experience to build for ourselves a beautiful life? Our brokenness didn't come to break us; on the contrary, it wants to make us better.

Maybe you've been tested in the fire of life. Be encouraged! Don't let the appearance of fire intimidate you. Know that as you are burned, you will not be destroyed. As you remain faithful in the process, God will determine your outcome. How we operate in the process will determine the product of our brokenness. Some people choose to become bitter, while others choose to be transformed into a good measure.

As you read these pages, be reminded that life is a gift to everyone, and you are living yours. Regardless of the pestilence you experience, it is your life, and you have what it takes to be victorious. In the ups and downs, don't give up! Look at brokenness as a perfectly positioned agent of God. Don't focus on the process that wants to break you; focus on God, who seeks to mold and make you. God knows what He is about, and He is about to do something amazing in your life.

May you be blessed!

ONE

YOU ARE NEVER ALONE

GOD IS WITH YOU

LONELINESS JUST DOESN'T feel good. If you've ever been alone, you'll understand what I mean by this. For a lonely person, it's like the world has forgotten about them. When not dealt with properly, this feeling can lead to toxic brokenness, as this combination of loneliness and brokenness can be life-threatening. Because of this, we should learn how to operate in these times. Regardless of our circumstances, faith is our perfect response. Our faithful response in these lonely moments is to know that we are never truly alone. Be reminded of this scripture found in Joshua 1:9: "*Have I not commanded you? Be strong and courageous. Do not be afraid; do not be discouraged, for the Lord your God will be with you wherever you go.*" God encourages Joshua to be confident in the fact that He (God) is with him. Joshua's victory was dependent on his faith.

As Joshua believed God, God was faithful to His promise toward him. Like Joshua, when we walk by faith, God is with us wherever we go. After God had blessed Joshua with His promise, He also comforted him with these encouraging words:

"*As I was with Moses, so I will be with you; I will never leave you nor forsake you*" (Joshua 1:5b). God's only requirement was for Joshua to be faithful and follow His Word. Joshua must have been boosted with great confidence when he heard these words: "I will be with you, *always*!"

One morning as I was getting ready for work, I was about to take something off my bookshelf when I suddenly looked up and saw my wallet hiding on top of the shelf in a little corner. At the angle where I stood I had a perfect view, yet had I been standing anywhere else, I never would have seen my wallet. When I saw it, I smiled at myself, because I knew I would have been looking for it all morning had I not seen it. In that moment, God whispered into my heart: "See, I am with you." I was comforted because I was going through a really lonely phase. At that time, life was so difficult, and it seemed like God had forgotten all about me.

The good news for us all is that in the midst of our brokenness, God is present with us, and as we follow His Word, He will be faithful to His promise. As we trust God, He will also grant us the desire of our heart. For the broken, the most notable desire is to be healed. Part of our healing is the knowledge that God is with us in every storm. A great king long ago knew this very well. David was a man with great anguish yet also great faith. As David was being scorched by the fire of life, he wrote this psalm: "*Where can I go from your Spirit? Where can I flee from your presence? If I go up to the heavens, you are there; if I make my bed in the depths, you are there*" (Psalm 139:7–9).

It's logical to think that if we have such a powerful Father and friend always walking with us, then we'll be safe from the troubles of life. But as we walk along, we soon realize that this isn't true. Troubles do come, and sometimes in great measure. Do these moments take away the great presence of God? No, they don't! On the contrary, they justify it. It's most often because of our brokenness that we get to experience the great miracles of God.

Along our broken roads, we must always remember that not everything that hurts us is harming us. Sometimes the hurt prevents us from being harmed. God in His wisdom knows exactly what He is doing. Be reminded as you walk with God that you are never alone, simply because God is with you— always!

> Along our broken roads, we must always remember that not everything that hurts us is harming us. Sometimes the hurt prevents us from being harmed.

HELP IS ALL AROUND US

Often in our brokenness, when our backs are against the wall, we feel alone. But as we learned from the previous section, scripture teaches that we are never truly alone because God is always with us wherever we go. We can never disregard the great importance of the resources around us that help us through our brokenness. By resources, I mean all the agents God has made available to us that can help us along our broken roads. These agents might be in the form of people, books, videos, etc., and they are carefully positioned to help us. Don't be afraid. As you walk by faith, receive the help God is sending to you.

The book of Genesis proves to us that human company is vital. When God made Adam, God saw that Adam had a need. God was always there with Adam, as were the animals, yet God saw that it wasn't good for Adam to be alone. When God saw Adam's need, He made a woman for him, who became his life partner. Whether it be our spouse, friends, or relatives, the company of good people is a beautiful and meaningful thing in our lives. In fact, true human company will exhibit the presence of God.

> *"The Lord God said, 'It is not good for the man to be alone. I will make a helper suitable for him"* (Genesis 2:18).

You shouldn't only surround yourself with good people but with good people who are relevant to your journeys. Not every good person is good for your situation. Often people who understand you are those who have been in your situation. People who have walked like you will understand the indelible, intimate wounds that can mar you along the way. These people have fought the battles you now face and overcame them by the grace of God. Perhaps God has given them the anointing to speak to your wounds, or maybe experience teaches wisdom, as the old saying goes.

We must ensure that we take deliberate action to surround ourselves with people who can help us. As we surround ourselves with the company of good people, let's also allow the mirror of understanding to decipher our needs. Sometimes it's in these healing spiritual sessions with people we trust that the deliverance we've been waiting on will appear. We shouldn't open ourselves to everyone, but we should open up ourselves to someone. We're often scared to share our problems with others, but I believe there are still trustworthy people who can listen to us and encourage us in the Lord.

One time I was going through a rough patch in my life, and God had placed a family member in my heart for me to reach out to. I knew that this relative could help me, but I was too prideful to reach out to him. Some time later, the same little problem became an even bigger one, and this time I was so broken, and my life so shattered, that I didn't hesitate to seek help. Consider how better it would have been had I sought help while the problem was still small.

God has put sufficient resources around us to support us in our needs. He considered all we would need to live a life of purpose and truth, and He has organized our surroundings to meet our needs. We just have to fill our needs with the provisions of God. Sometimes someone else's perspective is all we need. Many times you just need to hear from someone who can view the situation from a different angle or who has more experience.

God saw the lack of knowledge in the Israelites when He said, "*My people are destroyed from lack of knowledge*" (Hosea 4:6). Knowledge is the mastermind of truth. In John 8:32, Jesus says that you shall know the truth and the truth will set you free. As a result, we should seek the knowledge and wisdom from the resources around us. In your brokenness, be diligent in finding the courage to fight, and know that all things are beings worked out for your good.

"The truth is that a little problem that needs help will be a big problem that needs more help, if you do not seek help."

Love Walks with You

God is love, Love walks with you,
In hardest times, Love talks with you.
Love hovers you, Love paves your path,
He stays with you in the midst of wrath!

God is Love, Love abides yet still,
When the forces rage, they surrender to His will.
Love bothers you with goodness and grace,
Love walks with you in every place!

And Love is a Lion, the conquering One,
Love stays with you till the day is done …
And smiles with you, things Love will do,
Love rests with you as one that's true …

God is Love, and Love is kind,
God gives to you His very mind …
God is Love, and Love is true,
Love walks with you and talks with you!

GOD'S GRACE IS SUFFICIENT

Sufficient to the day are the troubles that come with it, yet sufficient to all our troubles is the sufficiency of Christ. As we walk with wounds, and as we talk with scars, let's always remember that we have grace that is sufficient for our needs. The Bible says that "*where sin abounded, grace did much more abound*" (Romans 5:20, KJV). Consider that God's grace abounds in our sinfulness, and then imagine how much more it will abound toward those who put their trust in Him.

I want you to believe that the Spirit of grace is sufficient for your brokenness. As I stated earlier, sometimes what we don't know affects us. It's important to know that as we are broken, there is healing through grace. The thing about grace is that we don't work for it. When we get paid for work, we call it a wage, but when we receive a free gift, that's grace. When I talk about the free gift of grace, I'm talking about the gift of endurance that keeps us going even when we feel like we're on empty. Often we will realize that it's not by our might or our power that we make it through our situations, but it's all through the grace of God.

Events will happen to us over which we have little to no control. In those times, we realize the importance of God's grace. These are the times when we should acknowledge and receive the grace at our disposal—the grace that is not a respecter of persons but is available to all who rely on it. It doesn't matter how complicated your circumstances may be—there is nothing more complicated than death, and God gives life over death. In the solitude of your broken place, duly rely on the grace of God, which is sufficient.

TWO
LIFE IS FULL OF SEASONS

IT'S JUST FOR A SEASON

SEASONS ARE LIKE spices that add value to our lives. "There is a season for everything," Solomon says, "a season to laugh and a season to cry, a season to love and a season to hate" (Ecclesiastes 3:1–8, paraphrased). Everything happens in the seasons we experience. What is happening to each of us at any given time is just us travelling through our seasons, trying to make it out. When we look at nature, we see four very distinct seasons, especially in certain parts of the world. There is nothing more beautiful than a bright spring morning in the back yards of Toronto, yet there is nothing more harsh than Canadian winter life (in Toronto). In this we see the same country, Canada, at different times, and in different states.

Each season comes with its own troubles and rewards. In the natural, according to scientists, summer weather offers warm conditions vital to the activities of animals, plants, and other living things. In winter, on the other hand, these same plants and animals have to retreat in search of summer warmth. God in His wisdom has made us like the seasons. Some seasons will challenge us into great grief. Other seasons will crucify us and destroy our very being. Each person experiences their own seasons, at their own times, in their own little spaces.

I once met a man who was very content with life, yet due to his contentment, he wasted his resources and his life. I met another man who was weary in well-doing because of his great grief. The big question is: "Which man is in the better position?" The Bible answers this question explicitly: "*Sorrow is better than laughter: for by the sadness of the countenance the heart is made better*" (Ecclesiastes 7:3, KJV). Not every situation we perceive as being bad is bad. Whatever situation makes us better is really better for us.

You might be going through the roughest season of your life, but never forget that this same rough season might be the most valuable one for you. In hard times we learn to be the strongest we can be, not because we have many choices, but because being strong is the only option we have in these times. Bob Marley said, "You never know how strong you are until being strong is the only option you have."[2] As you pass through the many seasons of life, let one thing remain—your faith in God that every little thing is going to be all right.

SORROW IS BETTER THAN LAUGHTER

Not all that appears bad is really bad for us. Not many people will experience growth in the good times, but I have seen many

[2] "Bob Marley Quotes," goodreads, accessed August 12, 2023, https://www.goodreads.com/quotes/884474-you-never-know-how-strong-you-are-until-being-strong

people catapult into destiny from the hardest of times. If we look deep into our own lives we will see that our worst times have left the most valuable lessons. The lessons we learn in the difficult times are ones that no amount of money can buy.

In Ecclesiastes 7:3, Solomon describes the beauty of sorrow (brokenness). He says that it's good for us to go through hard times. We should embrace these times with the knowledge that they are usually God moments and mean us no harm. It's so important to be faithful in perilous times. If we have no faith when we fall, then what we see will be limited to the level of our fall. Faith, however, allows us to see beyond our current level into the enormous levels-upon-levels that exist.

We should always try to see beyond what's happening to us now. One situation doesn't define or determine a life. We can be poor, but we must never remain poor. Poverty shouldn't be a permanent place. In a similar light, we may be broken, but we must never remain broken. Brokenness shouldn't be a permanent place.

Let's run the race that is before us, not always asking for better days but receiving what comes our way. Let's trust the hands of God, that they will give us what is necessary for our growth. In sorrowful days, let's give God praise, and in perilous times, let's pray!

> *"Therefore, since we are surrounded by such a great cloud of witnesses, let us throw off everything that hinders and the sin that so easily entangles. And let us run with perseverance the race marked out for us"* (Hebrew 12:1).

SEASONS COME WITH LESSONS

God is a man with a plan. In the book of Jeremiah, while speaking to the Israelites, God says, "*For I know the plans I have for you,' declares the Lord, 'plans to prosper you and not to harm you, plans to give you hope and a future*" (Jeremiah 29:11). God has a plan for your life, and His aim is to execute it by command of your faith.

> In your own struggles, you might not see the wisdom of God at work, but God is a Master Planner.

In your own struggles, you might not see the wisdom of God at work, but God is a Master Planner. He carefully delegates our circumstances as He sees fit. Let's not be distracted from the purpose of our situations. If we believe that the Lord is good, we must resolve to trust Him. Let's trust God when He places us in the dungeons of despair and on the pinnacle of peace.

We can learn a lot from the mother eagle as she deals with her young. As the young eaglet grows up, it must learn how to fly. For this to happen, the mother eagle must stir up the nest to create an uncomfortable situation. As the discomfort lingers, the eaglet will have no choice but to get out of that nest and get going. As the eaglet gets up, it spreads its wings in an attempt to fly. As it jumps from the nest, high in the sky, the mother eagle watches it with great precision. The moment the little one appears to be in danger, the mother eagle will be there to rescue it. Consider how God deals with us as His children. In like manner, we are watched as we advance into purpose, and the moment we're in danger, God rescues us with grace.

Maybe you're in a situation where God has stirred your nest. Take heart and don't worry. The same God who stirs your nest will catch you as you fall. As I wrote earlier, God is a Master Planner, and He knows exactly what He is up to.

Our job is to trust in the Lord with all our heart, leaning not on our own understanding, and to know that God directs our path. Don't let the seasons go by without learning the lessons they bring, but rather pay attention. Whatever you do as you stride through the seasons, and however hard life might get, don't give up! If you endure, you will live to see the glory of the Lord in the land of the living.

THIS TOO SHALL PASS

Nothing lasts forever. Time is a redeemer for us all. The scripture reads, "*For he says, 'In the time of my favor I heard you, and in the day of salvation I helped you.' I tell you, now is the time of God's favor, now is the day of salvation*" (2 Corinthians 6:2).

The right time is God's time, and this will shift the atmosphere of your life. Can you tell me of anything that lasts forever? The truth is, things always change. In our limited knowledge, we might not see through the cloudy darkness of this troubled world, yet God has an eternal lens and has set the boundaries of our pathway. Nothing can happen to us without God first giving it permission to happen, and things happen to us in the time God has allowed for them to happen. What is happening to us now as children of God is the thing that

God has approved in His divine wisdom. Our responsibility as we walk with God is to trust Him. Trusting God means that through thick and thin, we continue to press on and look to Him.

I often look back at my life and consider that though I've gone through a lot of situations, they have all passed, and God has rescued me out of them all. There's not one situation in my life up to this day that God hasn't helped me through, except the one He is now bringing me through. We must use the history of God's goodness as evidence that He will always be faithful to us. When we're bombarded with circumstances, we often forget about the great goodness of our God, but God is always good, and great is His goodness to those who trust in Him. Let's wholly and fully trust God and that as He brings us to life, He will also bring us through life. If you're hurt with no sense of direction, I want you to know that it's just for a season, and this too shall pass. Be empowered beyond your brokenness, and as you move along, remember that our seasons add spice to our lives. Never give up!

THREE
THE POWER OF BROKENNESS

THERE IS POWER IN OUR BROKENNESS

THE WORD "POWER" denotes ability and authority. If I say I have power, it means I have the capacity and authority to achieve my set objectives. Similarly, if I say I have power in my brokenness, it means I have the capacity and the authority to overcome it. I have found that there is great power in the solitudes of a broken place. Something tends to happen when we're broken. It's often in the bottomless pit of a broken place that we learn life's greatest lessons. I speak about the power of brokenness in the sense that without our brokenness, there is nothing much to learn.

The Bible speaks of Job, a faithful servant yet a broken individual. Job said in his pain, "*Though he slay me, yet will I hope in him*" (Job 13:15). He went further to say, "*when he has tried me, I shall come out as gold*" (Job 23:10b, ESV). We should understand that God is the great judge of our lives and that He is for us, not against us. When God tries us in a broken place, His intentions aren't to harm us but to give us a future and a hope.

It's inevitable that we'll be broken at times, as whom the Lord loves, He corrects. Most often in the process of God transforming us, we will have to be broken. God does what is necessary and good for us, not what's convenient and comfortable. For God, it's better for us to enter into His kingdom broken than not to enter at all. Similarly, it's better for us to enter the kingdom of God missing many pieces than not to enter at all. When we understand this, we will realize the wisdom that God works out in our situations.

We must enter the kingdom, so we must be broken! We must also be broken away from yesterday so that we can cling to the power and victory of tomorrow.

BROKENNESS IS A PREREQUISITE

The Bible reads: *"because the Lord disciplines the one he loves, and he chastens everyone he accepts as his son"* (Hebrews 12:6). This scripture explains what I mean by brokenness being a pre-requisite. Consider Paul, a man of heavenly origins yet a man who was severely broken. Paul was one of the greatest contributors to the Bible, having written most of the New Testament. Amidst such a high revelation, he remained a very broken person. Paul was so broken that he cried out to God to remove thorns from his flesh (2 Corinthians 12:7–8). For Paul, no amount of revelation could prevent him from being torn apart. As Paul cried to God, God responded by saying, *"My grace is sufficient for you, for my power is made perfect in your weakness"* (2 Corinthians 12:9a).

In order for us to experience the perfect power of God, we must be broken. Think of brokenness as the divine method of God. It doesn't matter who we are, where we're from, or who we're affiliated with. Brokenness happens to the best of us. The good news is that we have what it takes to endure our brokenness, so we must endure. When Paul the apostle petitioned God, he realized that in his weakness, the power of God was being worked out. Paul also knew that it was in his brokenness that the power of God was being perfected in him. You should be careful not to stop the flow of God's power. The brokenness we often endure is just the spring that will push us forward. As we experience the tension of a broken place, we should understand that it is brewing power within us.

If you've ever used a slingshot, you'll understand the power of tension. Remember that King David used the tension from a slingshot to kill the great giant Goliath. The power that lies within the tension of your brokenness can catapult you further than any other thing could even come close to doing.

THERE IS VALUE IN BROKENNESS

It's quite fascinating to watch the trees as they spread into the sky. I believe we can learn a lot from the trees and plants in general. A tree is the result of a seed dying. A seed must be planted and decay, and from the decay of a seed, the new life of a plant begins. We can identify with the enormous value plants possess. They're used for energy, lumber, and food, among many other uses. What started in the brokenness of decay results in the sprout of life. The value of a tree is priceless. Consider us like a grain of seed that must be broken in order to become so valuable that we are priceless.

In the book of John, Jesus speaks about the power of brokenness in the life of a seed: "*Verily, verily, I say unto you, Except a corn of wheat fall into the ground and die, it abideth alone: but if it die, it bringeth forth much fruit*" (John 12:24, KJV).

Jesus is saying here that a broken seed produces value. Consider the Lord as He was led to the cross. It is written that He was wounded for our transgressions and bruised for our iniquities (Isaiah 53:5). Isaiah goes on to state that the punishment of our peace was upon Him. If God saw it fit to chasten His own son in order to save us, how much more will He break us in order to make us.

We should submit ourselves to the will of God for our lives. There is absolutely nothing more important than the purpose of God for us, and to reach the place of our divine calling, we must be transformed through brokenness. As we do this, God will add value to our situations. It is often said "He will turn your mess into a message." Trust in God!

BROKENNESS IS BURDEN-LIFTING

When we look at brokenness through eyes of faith, we see yet another treasure. Our brokenness has the ability to lighten our loads. At one point in my life, I was immersed in unforgiveness. For me, unforgiveness was my right. I had the right to hold a grudge against the person who did me wrong. I wrestled with unforgiveness for quite a while, and my brokenness became unbearable, to a point where I had to let it go. When enough is enough, something has to change.

When the pain from our brokenness becomes greater than the pleasure or security of holding to it, then we tend to let go. I was so broken that I had to be healed. My healing was in the treasuries of my brokenness, because after a while, enough was enough. Have you ever been in a position where enough was enough? We are seeds, and seeds don't permanently die. There's a Mexican proverb that goes like this: "They tried to bury me, but they didn't know I was a seed." Brokenness is actually good for a seed, because as stated earlier, through the brokenness of decay, a seed will result in the sprout of life. Like a caterpillar, a seed will change from one state to the next. Seeds change through death, as much as we change through resurrection power.

I finally realized that there had to be a better way. I yearned for a happy day in the spoils of my own grief. The prodigal son must have experienced something very similar. He wandered away from home—far, far away. As he wandered, he became so lost and broken that enough was enough. Sometimes enough has to be enough for us to finally let go and let God. Finally, the prodigal son went home where he belonged. His brokenness drove him home.

For many, it was in their most broken states when they finally reached the bottom of the bottomless pit of despair, and then they finally looked up and saw Christ looking down. In Matthew 11:28, Jesus says, "*Come to me, all you who are weary and burdened, and I will give you rest.*" Through Jesus Christ, there is rest for the broken. From the trails of a broken way, we learn how to let go and let God.

BROKEN PIECES BUILD A BEAUTIFUL COLLAGE

I can't say this enough: brokenness can be beautiful. We will never know the beauty of our brokenness until we organize our broken pieces into a beautiful collage. Consider the birds, how they use broken branches to build their homes. For a broken person, it might be using the pieces of a broken life to bless others in need. It doesn't matter your situation, your brokenness can be used to beautify the lives of others and the world.

Our modern society teaches us to discard broken stuff. If our car is broken, we discard it; if our marriages are broken, we do the same. This mentality isn't good for any society because what would have been our strength, we discard. It's the beauty of our brokenness that teaches us to challenge the future with boldness. Broken paths might be narrow and lonely, but they lead to beautiful destinations. It is written that narrow is the gate that leads to heaven (Matthew 7:14), and for the broken person, narrow is the way that leads to their healing.

Through our brokenness, we gain valuable experiences. In an imperfect world shattered with sin, brokenness is an everyday reality. When the body is sick, we go to the doctor, and when the spirit is sick, we should seek a spiritual doctor. Broken spirits need a doctor of the spirit. God is that doctor. Imagine how beautiful our lives will become when we allow our God, the doctor of the spirit, to use our brokenness to build something beautiful.

The Bible says that Jesus could have called ten thousand angels to rescue Him from going to the cross. Yet the brokenness of the cross was the most important piece of the story of salvation. We might wonder why God chose to lead Jesus down this broken road, but as I said before, broken roads lead to beautiful destinations. As Jesus was led to the cross, He was being led into victory. As you face your own dilemma, God will also lead you into victory as you trust Him.

The power of brokenness is the wisdom of God. God knows the residue of power left in the person who faithfully endures his or her brokenness. As Paul endured his brokenness, God's power was being perfected in him (2 Corinthians 12:8–10). Job had a similar experience as he was submerged in his anguish. The Bible says that he uttered, "*But he knows the way that I take; when he has tested me, I will come forth as gold*" (Job 23:10). Gold is purified by fire, and we are the golden pieces of God. We should be faithful like Job, who even in the fire praised God.

As we juggle with the broken pieces of our lives, let's be keen to make use of them. Remember that in all of what you go through, God is trying to make you a better human being. Be empowered as you team with God to build a beautiful life.

IN THE PUDDLE OF DESPAIR

In the puddle of despair,
I know my God is near.
For He walks beside me,
And He'll forever guide me.

Way in the puddle of despair,
I know He goes before me.
And though this fire burns my hair,
The Lord is a shelter for me!

I'll sing praises in this puddle,
Here in this puddle cuddle.
I make paddles in this muddle,
In this puddle, as I huddle!

Yet I find cradle in this puddle,
This puddle of despair!
As I huddle in this muddle,
I know my God is near!

BROKENNESS BRINGS US CLOSER TO GOD

I believe that whatever brings us closer to God is good for us. It's not the best circumstances that will do this, but it's those uncomfortable, uneasy moments that will bring us to our knees. As we are broken, and as our pieces fall apart, let's use this opportunity to move closer to the One who can help us. In the depths of our gullies, we often find the need to look to the hills from where we receive our help. This hill is the hill of God!

We never see change without some form of friction. When something is to be formed, it often must go through very high or low temperatures in order to test and authenticate its quality. A car will go through intense crash tests to ensure it's safe on the road, and God places us in the high temperatures of complex situations to authenticate us. Remember Job as he underwent the fire of the goldsmith and potter. In Job's torment, he knew that all things would work together for his good.

Sometimes our brokenness is there to keep us humble, yet due to our limited understanding, we might not see this. Due to the intense hurts that come with brokenness, we often think that our brokenness has come to hurt us. I have better news for you. Whatever you're going through, no matter how hard life may get, we have the choice to be broken or to be built. Be built!

BROKENNESS RIDS PRIDE

Growing up, I was very judgemental. Like most of us, I thought that when people didn't meet my expectations, they were bad, and I would never do those things myself. As I grew older, I realized that given time and circumstances, we all fall short. I realized that I wasn't perfect and that I had the capacity to be as bad as my neighbour. Jesus stated in Matthew 7:5, "*You hypocrites, first take the plank out of your own eye, and then you will see clearly to remove that speck from your brother's eye."* We should approach to help others not from a place of judgement but from a place of love.

As I grew older, all I held to I had to let go. I was very prideful because I was ignorant. I had confidence in my flesh because I lacked the experience of a broken place. What I realized is that I can be the liar, the cheater, and the unforgiving one. As I began to see my own weakness, I looked away and saw the perfection of Christ. I started to lower my expectations of self and let go of the pillars of pride that were set up in my life. I found out that my perfection was in the person of Jesus Christ.

When we begin to see ourselves for who we really are, we begin to look away from self in total disgust. Let self be slain and let God be glorified. The one who comes into the bright and astronomical light of the truth will see. He will be free because he will see both his wretchedness and God's light. When this happens, we look away from our self-filth in scorn, and we look to the purity of our God. I can't overemphasize that our brokenness is not necessarily bad for us, because when see through eyes of faith, we see that our brokenness points heavenward.

BROKENNESS WILL INEVITABLY CHANGE US

Anyone who has ever experienced true brokenness will know that when you pass through those troubled seas, you can't come out the same. You'll either come out better or more bitter. This has to do with both how we view our brokenness and how we operate while we experience it. Brokenness will turn up the heat to the point where we become molten in the fiery furnace of life. Fire has the ability to purify us and also to destroy us. As a result, the key to our survival in the fiery furnace of this life is to seek positive change while expecting and waiting for it.

Let us be like Shadrach, Meshach, and Abednego, who replied to King Nebuchadnezzar:

> *If we are thrown into the blazing furnace, the God we serve is able to deliver us from it, and He will deliver us from your majesty's hand. But even if He does not, we want you to know, Your Majesty, that we will not serve your gods or worship the image of gold you have set up.* (Daniel 3:17–18)

We should expect to live to see the miracle of God in our lives. The truth is, the thing we expect to happen is the thing we have faith in. If we expect a bad outcome for our life, then we have faith in that bad outcome. On the contrary, if we expect God's goodness, then we have faith in the goodness of God.

> We should expect to live to see the miracle of God in our lives.

The scriptures admonish us to wait on the Lord: "*Wait on the Lord: be of good courage, and he shall strengthen thine heart: wait, I say, on the Lord*" (Psalm 27:14, KJV). As we are broken, let's remain faithful to the very end. We must consider our brokenness as an agent of God that seeks to make us better. It really doesn't matter the position we're in—brokenness can make us better. The good being worked out in us is so necessary that it's profitable for us to go through it. Most often, the thing that God is breaking us from is far worse for our life than the pain of breaking us away.

As seasons change, you won't remain the same forever. One day you'll look back at the memory of a broken yesterday and smile at the beauty it painted in you. You'll suddenly realize that God knew what He was about each step of the way. Be encouraged in your brokenness. Allow your broken road to lead you to a beautiful place.

FOUR

PRAYING THROUGH YOUR BROKENNESS

PRAYER HEALS OUR BROKENNESS

PRAYER IS AN essential activity we must practise as we travel through our broken places. Prayer is the gift God gave us to help us through the evil that wants to attack us while we are broken. In our grief, it's perhaps the hardest time to pray, yet it's the most essential time to go before the throne of God. Our brokenness can bring us to a place of great hurt, which can breed hate in our hearts. But the power that comes from our prayerful praise will empower us in these times to shed this weight of sin and to chose the way of God.

There was a time when I was so broken that all sorts of thoughts were flowing through my mind. These thoughts were both good and bad. When we're hurt, we become quite vulnerable to both the good and the evil forces around us. Our vulnerability also exposes us to the cowardly attacks of Satan, who is both a coward and an opportunist (also an ignorant fool) who attacks us in our weakness. Yet it's in this same weakness that we experience the transforming power of God through prayer. I felt betrayed, as I was lied to and wrongly accused by someone close, and all I wanted to do was take matters into my own hands. I wanted to fight fire with fire.

But when we add fire to fire, we breed more fire, and too much fire will burn down a building. We are the buildings of the Most High God, and if we allow the fire of sin to penetrate us, this same building of God will burn into the building of Satan. We must choose the narrow way of prayer, but this is not an easy task to accomplish, as every nerve in you will seek recompense for the wrong done to you. But no amount of vengeful thinking can take away the truth of God—that the effective and fervent prayer of the righteous avails much. Our job here is to be faithful in order to keep our righteousness intact.

As Paul the apostle cried out to God in his own weakness, the Bible says that God didn't take away his suffering; rather, He strengthened him through it. This doesn't mean that God will never rid us of our brokenness, but brokenness must have its perfect work. There is a time when brokenness is the most valuable thing for us, and this might be you doing your time. The key is to dwell in constant prayer and, like Paul, to listen and follow the voice of God.

Brokenness doesn't feel good, and we seek to get out of it as soon as possible. Some people use substances to alleviate the pain, while others seek revenge, yet the greatest antidote is to pray. Given time, payer, and faith, God will keep us and heal us through our brokenness. There is a power we can appeal to that will help us in our infirmities. As Paul did, let's dwell in constant prayer.

PRAYER BRINGS US CLOSER TO OUR HEALING

Prayer brings us closer to God, who is the source of our healing. In our brokenness, our need tumbles us to our knees. While this is true, many people chose other things, such as alcohol and drugs, to help them through their hurts, not recognizing the healing power of prayer. Yet the Bible says that we should pray for one another that we may be healed.

During times of brokenness, the most valuable thing for us to do is to petition our God who heals (Jehovah Rapha). In this time, prayer isn't only good for our spiritual health, but it also has the power to heal our physical bodies. Prayer, when mixed with faith, is the antidote we require to heal our broken hearts and bind our wounds. The Psalmist said it like this: "*He heals the brokenhearted and binds up their wounds*" (Psalm 147:3).

As we pass through a broken place, it might hurt us so badly that we begin to deteriorate both in body and in mind, yet we often have to become less to be more. In the natural, this makes very little sense, yet the laws of the flesh can't sufficiently explain the laws of the spirit. This is perhaps why in the natural it's hard to identify with the power of prayer. Nonetheless, those who pray will be the ones who go the distance.

As we are broken, we should carry a perpetual prayer in our hearts. In fact, our lives should become prayers. As we do this, God will not only heal us, but He will show us the

> As we are broken, we should carry a perpetual prayer in our hearts. In fact, our lives should become prayers.

29

way to go. It's through the intimate sessions of prayer that God directs our paths.

MY PRAYER IS MY PRAISE
My prayer will be my praise,
For the entirety of my days.
And it's my weapon,
This is what I reckon!

That my prayer will go before me,
And petition for me.
To the One up above,
My prayer will appease His love.

Prayer, it lifts me higher,
It's my pouring of fire!
That helps me in my place,
And appeals to heaven's grace.

I will pray perpetually,
Into the realm of eternity!
It's my prayer, my praise,
For the rest of my days!

DWELL IN CONSTANT PRAYER
Never stop praying. Don't allow the bulb of your prayer to go dim. Your only source of strength in your brokenness is God, and the way to reach God is to pray; therefore, let your praise be

a prayer. God will never get tired of hearing your voice; in fact, He loves to hear you.

As you pray, you should also believe. Believe that the best will happen as you pray. It's easy to give in, in the innermost parts of the fire of life, but you must build spiritual stamina through your faithful prayers. Know that God is for you, and that as you pray, He is opening new doors and closing dormant ones. There will be days when you become so low that you don't even know what to pray, but let your heart pray for you. God knows your heart, and He hears it. In these times you should also let the Spirit of God intercede for you. The Bible says that the Holy Spirit makes intercession for us with groanings that cannot be spoken out loud (Romans 8:26). This means that when we become speechless, our faith will trigger the Spirit of intercession to pray for us. Our job is to be faithful in our utmost intercessions and to perpetually pray.

"Likewise the Spirit also helpeth our infirmities: for we know not what we should pray for as we ought: but the Spirit itself maketh intercession for us with groanings which cannot be uttered" (Romans 8:26, KJV).

DOING THE RIGHT THING

We aren't exempt from divine duties as we seek to be healed by the grace of God. One of the very important things that we must do as we are broken is to do what is right. Even in the case where we have to endure a little longer, as Paul did, we still have to do the righteous thing in order to find the strength to endure. In Paul's case, God was perfecting His power in him as he endured the thorn in his flesh. The weakness that we go through, and the broken vessels we result in, are just us becoming less for God to become more.

God wants to heal us, but our healing comes from us becoming less for God to become more. In this way, God can live in us, and we can be love, as He is. Remember that God is love, and love never fails. Think about it for a little while: *God is love, and love never fails.* Imagine if we practised true love! The Bible says love keeps no record of wrongs. This means that we must do the right thing, which is to let go and to forgive fully. If we do this, the scripture will be fulfilled in our lives: "*Love never fails*" (1 Corinthians 13:8). We must understand that we never fail if we never give up. The goal is to reach the prize, and our prize is to be transformed into the full measure of God. For this to happen, we must do the right thing.

In our brokenness, we are left shattered for the most part, and we often hold to the deceitful comfort of grudge. When we hold grudge, we hold to the pain of yesterday. The grudge is nothing more than us holding to the painful memory of what we've gone through. We must let go of this, and we must know that today is the new day that the Lord has made, and we should rejoice and be glad in it. I implore you to do the right thing, even little by little. It will sometimes take a little while for you to fully die to yourself, but if you can't do it in one day, do it little by little each day. By God's grace, you can do what is right as you endure through your brokenness.

FIVE

DON'T GIVE UP

NEVER GIVE UP

PRESS! STRIDE TOWARD the finish line. As you go about life's great mission, find the courage to endure your fight. In our brokenness, when our pieces are all falling apart, our apparent escape is to cease from dealing with what's going on. We tend to want to give up when the pain becomes unbearable. But when we don't deal with what's going on, it keeps going on. As we travel, let's realize that the only way out is the way through.

A man who uses drugs to get rid of his problems will always recover from his high with the same problems. If he doesn't deal with what's happening and face his problems head-on, he can never make it through. He must soberly challenge his circumstances, even to the point of death. I believe that it's better to die while trying than to not try at all. Therefore, let us die while trying so that we die a heroic death. I travel with this one thought: Even if I die in my troubles, I have the power of resurrection to raise me up from any dead place. I have the Way. I have the Truth. I have the Life.

As I write, I consider my own journey, having been so broken that I wanted to give up so badly. I've tried to give up on many occasions. I wanted to give up mainly because it was too painful to continue. Somehow, however, I find strength in my weakness that keeps me going on. I call this grace. This undeserved power comes from the hands of God. It doesn't come because I'm strong, or overly powerful, but it has always been through the Spirit of God that I am able to endure.

Many times it's not enough to say that you will never give up, because this has to be followed by a steadfast mind and a strong will to go on. We can learn a lot from the Bible about not giving up. Philippians 3:14 contains these famous words of the Apostle Paul: "*I press on toward the goal to win the prize for which God has called me heavenward in Christ Jesus.*" Paul pressed. The very act of pressing is a signal that there is opposition. In the midst of this opposition, when our muscles get weary and our stench stains, giving up can be a heart's best friend. But not all best friends are good friends. It's always a good thing for you when you make the decision that it doesn't matter how hard life gets or how insurmountable your paths may become, you will never give up. If we die along the way, resurrection power will resuscitate us. Keep going and never give up!

Maybe you're broken. Don't give up. You might be dealing with a broken person, but with the same measure, you should never give up. You might be so emotionally unstable that you keep hurting the people you love, bearing constant regret. In this situation, you should seek help, but you can never give up. Continue to press, knowing that there is hope for the broken.

The Bible says that a broken and a contrite heart the Lord loves (Psalm 51:17). Dear broken, look to the Lord with openness, willing to confess your wrong, and watch the Lord feed you with His faithfulness.

SINGULAR

In a singular world, I am a singular being,
At a singular time, I'm a singular stream.
I'm a singular beam that shines the earth,
And I'm the product of many, many, many, many hurt!

Yet in a singular sphere, I have a singular hope,
That God is always by me as I cope.
For in a singular pain is a singular space,
I cling to a one and a singular grace …

I have a singular cry, with a singular creed,
A singular heart, with a singular need.
Yet on a singular way Christ walks with me,
On a singular line He talks with me.

I'm a singular man, I'm a singular son,
A singular plan, on a singular run.
Oh who is me, I'm a one undone,
I'm a singular strain under the sun.

In a singular world, I'm a singular beam,
At a singular time, in a singular stream.

GIVING UP SHOULD NOT BE AN OPTION

When we eliminate the option to give up, we most often won't give up. Usually wedding vows include the words "for better or worse, for richer or poorer, in sickness and in health, till death do us part." This vow is very admirable, for it eliminates the option of giving up. When we make up our minds that until death we will keep going, then we tend to keep going.

Are we able to make a similar vow, that through thick and thin, through hell and high waters, no matter how hard it gets, we will never give up? I believe that we owe it to ourselves to make this vow. We deserve to achieve what we have set out to achieve, and we most certainly deserve to be all that God has made us to be.

The only way to our destination, however, is on the path that we can never give up. So often we stand in our own way. Our pride will lead to our greatest demise. Let go of self and do it. Self will offer us safety and security, but faith will offer us true hope and eternity.

There's a popular story about Hernan Cortes, an army general who burnt his ships. Upon arriving in the new world with about six hundred men, Cortez gave the instructions to burn the ships upon reaching land. This way the soldiers had no other alternative but to move forward. I find that when we as humans have no other alternative but to be strong, we will be strong. The great Bob Marley once said, "You can never know how strong you are until being strong is the only option you have."[3] Some years later, after burning his ships, Hernan Cortes succeeded in his conquest and claimed victory.

Take some time and look back at your own life. Consider if there has even been a situation that you thought would kill you but, through faith and determination, you found the strength to endure and to succeed. When strength is our only option, we tend to be strong, and when advancing forward is our only hope, we will conquer and advance.

I migrated to Canada earlier in my life. Before I migrated, I made up my mind that whatever happened as I ventured to the unknown, I would keep going. Before I left my homeland of Jamaica, I had a good job and was starting to see light in my career. I was a successful young professional with a bright future. I knew that the decision I was about to make would be a hard one, but I also felt that this decision was very important in the purpose of my life. I sold everything I had and gave up my job. I burnt every bridge that would give me a crossing back home and made sure it would be harder to return than to stay in Canada.

When I moved to Canada, I thought I'd made the worst decision one could ever make. Emotionally, I was crucified daily. I was broken to the point of suicidal thoughts. I wanted to get it over with, but I just couldn't die. A few years later, I looked back and realized that I'd made it through. I wasn't stronger than the man who gave up, but it was all in the decision

---

[3] Donald Smith, "Sometimes It's Best to Burn Your Ships," ME&A, September 7, 2022, https://www.meandahq.com/sometimes-its-best-to-burn-your-ships/.

I made to never give up, by the grace of God. I eliminated the option of quitting, so the only other option I had was to keep going. Many of the things I can say about brokenness come as a result of my time in Canada. Canada might not have been a permanent place, but it left a permanent mark on me—a mark of hope through brokenness.

> It's wonderful to know that not even death can steal away a soul committed to never giving up. Be strong and never give up.

I want to implore you to do the same. Whatever path God is leading you on, commit to continue and to never give up. Burn your ships and get rid of every avenue that would give you a path of escape. Inevitably, you will travel through a broken place at some point in your life, especially as you decide to follow the way of God. It's wonderful to know that not even death can steal away a soul committed to never giving up. Be strong and never give up.

YOU HAVE WHAT IT TAKES

There's a popular story about a lion who got lost among some sheep. Growing up with the sheep, this lion behaved like a sheep, ate like a sheep, and had no idea it was really a lion. The lion thought it was a sheep, but that didn't make it a sheep. Once a lion, always a lion. You don't become a sheep by acting like a sheep and eating with other sheep. You're a sheep when you're born a sheep. Your identity is in the image you were created in and has nothing to do with what you think and feel about who you are or who you should be. Although the lion thought it was a sheep, when met with danger, the lion came out. Isn't it the same with us? There is hidden strength that is only found when the situation demands it.

Our true potential isn't realized in fair weather but rather in high turbulence, when the strong northerly winds are against us. One day the lion met with an older lion who brought it to a pond to show it who it really was. When the young lion saw its image and came into identity with its true self, it roared in self actualization. The young lion found an energy it never had before, and from that day, the lion never again acted like a sheep.

Hidden within us is the ability to overcome the trials we are put in. This is because as a wise builder, God has given us all it takes for us to endure and overcome. Like the young lion, we often act like sheep. Many of us grew up around people who acted like sheep, and eventually we also began to act like sheep. It's in the moments that demand the lion in us that the lion really comes out. When we're met with circumstances that only lions can handle, we will come to terms with the lion within us. We are products of the conquering Lion of the Tribe of Judah. Let's act like lions, because indeed we are.

Often it's through the cracks of our brokenness that the hidden energy or our lion nature escapes. In Ecclesiastes 7:29, we read, "*Lo, this only I have found, that God hath made man upright; but they have sought out many inventions*" (KJV). God made us upright, but sin has corrupted us. Initially we were made precious jewels. Over the years, we get covered in all sorts of filth and baggage. Filth and baggage don't take away our identity—they just hide it. The moment we come to terms with who we really are, then we will roar in our divine place. Deep under the skins of our brokenness lies our true self. Sometimes we must be broken and our pieces fall apart, not to break us but to reveal our true self. In your brokenness, be faithful, be patient, be bold, and be brave, and you must never give up! Always remember, you have what it takes.

IT IS GOD'S WILL FOR YOU TO ENDURE

God is cheering for you! Amidst the many enemies that you face, and the insurmountable struggles you experience, God is right there as a cloud of witness, cheering for you to endure. In the midst of what you're going through, God is right there to help you get through it. The key thing is for you to endure in the purpose of God. As you endure, you will experience the presence of God pressing you on.

Life is like a bargain. If you fulfill your end of the deal, God will fulfill His end. This means that you have to approach the presence of God faithfully, with a clean and a pure heart, as it requires a clean heart to go before God. The Bible says that only those with clean hands and a pure heart can enter into the hills of our God. As a result, we must lay down the weight of sin that keeps us from experiencing the power and presence of God. When we do this, we have the full backing of our strong God.

Hebrew 12:1–2a says:

Therefore, since we are surrounded by such a great cloud of witnesses, let us throw off everything that hinders and the sin that so easily entangles. And let us run with perseverance the race marked out for us, fixing our eyes on Jesus, the pioneer and perfecter of faith.

For the broken, you might be loaded with the burdens of yesterday. Consider going forward with a constant heavy load, and imagine how much further you would reach if you never had this load. When we live in the past, we constantly travel with a heavy load. The Bible says that we should lay this load aside. It's easy to travel with the constant heavy load of a past we can't change, but it's also a medium for sin. We must learn from the past, but we must never live in it. Living in the past is like slowly drinking poison every day.

At one time in my life I drank this poison daily. I was engulfed in the walls of yesterday. I was so lured in that it began to affect most areas of my life. My emotions were all over the place, my energy was low, and I was very easily angered. As I struggled in this state, I found that this burden was too heavy for me. I realized that I couldn't go forward because I was carrying a load that was too heavy for me. I had to let go! As you let go, remember that God wants to push you forward, and you are the only person who can stand in your way.

GOD HONOURS A CLEAN AND RIGHTEOUS HEART

Brokenness can shadow our eyes from seeing the great presence of God with us, but it's essential for us to see the fingerprints of God in every part of our lives. As the children of God, we might fall seven times, but we will rise again through the grace and power of the Almighty God. Sometimes we fall so deep that we might think that we're permanently submerged, but God is able to reach us in our deepness and deliver us by His grace. His grace is sufficient for us.

You might have done so much wrong, yet your wrong doesn't take away the mercy and grace of God. Often in our brokenness we do things we regret and that have lasting impacts on us, such as unforgiveness, anger, hate, and hurt, which will slowly kill us both physically and spiritually. For God to help us, we must cultivate a clean and pure heart. This means letting go of all the weights of sin and taking on the person of God. As we do this, God will honour the cleanliness of our hearts and heal us.

SIX

FORGIVENESS IS NECESSARY

LET GO OF YESTERDAY

SOONER OR LATER, we'll realize that forgiveness is necessary if we want to proceed. As we are broken, a main prerequisite for us to move forward is to let go of yesterday. This means forgiving the people who have done us wrong and, most importantly, forgiving ourselves. If we allow it, we will perpetually live in yesterday. Yesterday's pain can leave such a stubborn stain that we are marred for life. Many times the chains of yesterday never seem to want to let us go. The shackles of the past often last, and yesterday can become the most toxic place. Yet it makes little sense to hold to the hells of yesterday.

Hebrew 12:1 reads, "*Therefore, since we are surrounded by such a great cloud of witness, let us throw off everything that hinders and the sin that so easily entangles. And let us run with perseverance the race marked out for us.*" The writer is being very specific about the things that hinder and the sin that entangles us. Yesterday can leave some very obvious marks, yet in order for us to move forward, we have to let these scars go.

Consider the one who has been sexually exploited. Imagine the pain of this memory each time it crosses this person's mind. If you haven't been there, you might not fully understand, but broken hearts are hard to heal. This is especially true when the people closest to us have caused us the harm. Often it's our closest companions who are able to hurt us the most, simply because we trust them the most. Yet no matter the hurt or where it comes from, it's important to let go of the things that hinder us.

More detrimental than these things are the sins that hold us back. In order to move forward, we must let go of these sins. It's easy to harbour grudges from a broken yesterday. Unforgiveness will often be the broken's best friend. Hate, envy, and anger are just some of the sins we often hold close. The thing about sin is that it's a really heavy load, and a broken person with a heavy load can never go far. In order for us to advance into the future, we must let go of the past.

PICKING UP THE PIECES

Our brokenness often leaves us in pieces. As we walk in the tracks of our cross, we are broken, battered, marred, and wounded from the issues of life. Though so horrendous, our brokenness will have to be healed. If the broken is to be healed, the pieces that fell apart need to be put back together or discarded altogether. The beauty about our brokenness is that we get to decide what pieces to keep and which ones to throw away. The Apostle Paul puts it this way: "*Brethren, I count not myself to have apprehended: but this one thing I do, forgetting those things which are behind, and reaching forth to those things that are before*" (Philippians 3:13, KJV). Paul is saying here that there are some things we have to let go of.

There are unnecessary pieces that we must leave behind. Kelly Clarkson's song "Piece by Piece" explains this scenario well. Clarkson has had a very broken past, coming from a broken home from childhood and then advancing into a broken marriage. She knows what it's like to be broken into shambles. The song speaks of a husband who collected her piece by piece, a husband who, after holes left from her past and a father leaving, collected her pieces and put her back together. This is the story of the broken, stripped, and disassembled, yet after a while put back together by a Saviour. Our story as a people of God is about people broken by sin who have been perfectly reassembled by a caring God.

ACCEPT AND GO

It's important to identify with where we're at. Yes, you might be broken, and you might be travelling in pieces, but it is what it is, and you must accept this reality and move on. At times I've regretted the past so bad that it began to hurt me. I made a decision earlier in my life that I was warned against, yet I went on to do it anyway. Later on I found out that this was really a bad decision, but at that point I couldn't undo it. For years I lived in constant regret. I used to just sit, looking out in space and wondering to myself how in the world had I made this decision. But no amount of regret could undo what was done. All I was doing was hurting myself thinking that regret could take away the pain. It took me years to accept the past for what it was, to find peace in my present, and then to move on to brighter days. Don't make the same mistake that I made and live in regret for years. The sooner you accept the past, the sooner you release the great future God has in store for your life.

In order to move on, you must let go of what's behind, and in order to let go, you have to accept that it is what it is. There comes a time when you have to accept responsibility for all that you are, what you've been through, the things you've done, and the paths you've taken. Your current reality is a sum total of all the things for which you need to take responsibility.

> In order to move on, you must let go of what's behind, and in order to let go, you have to accept that it is what it is.

You might be warring with yourself, as I did for years, but now is the time to let go. Any moment can initiate change, because change has to be initiated in a moment. If you don't start to change, you can never change. The place to start is the place of acceptance, where you come to terms with the reality that this is who you are, and this is what you've been through. When you come into acceptance, you relieve yourself of the guilt and the burdens of a past you can never change.

Every man has his own struggles, and every woman has her own pains, and even the little child cries in an unknown tongue tears that appeal to heaven. We're all in this together, and the sooner we realize that victories and defeats belong to us all, the sooner we conquer defeat and rise up. Not even death will have the power to imprison a resurrected soul that comes to terms with his or her eternal being.

"Get up, stand up," the great game-changer Nester Marley once sang, "stand up for your right." You have the right to prosper and be of good health. You must be the one you envision, and you must challenge the odds to solidify the power of God in your life. You have been given the power to unwrap the one you envision. What are you waiting on? Resist the fear that will always be there and see the faith that will bring you through destiny's gate. Arise, take up your bed, and walk!

SEVEN

THE COMPLEXITY OF BROKENNESS

BROKEN PEOPLE ARE DEEPLY BROKEN

HANNAH, A WOMAN from the Bible, was broken. She wanted children but had none, for the Bible tells us that God had closed Hannah's womb. Amidst this, Hannah's prayer was a praise unto God.

After many times pleading to God, Hannah's brokenness began to show. The prophet Eli saw her in her lamentation and thought she was drunk:

> *"Not so, my lord," Hannah replied, "I am a woman who is deeply troubled. I have not been drinking wine or beer; I was pouring out my soul to the Lord. Do not take your servant as a wicked woman; I have been praying here out of my great anguish and grief."* (1 Samuel 1:15)

This scripture sums it all up: Hannah was so broken that she appeared drunk. Have you ever been so broken that you even appeared drunk? Did you slur your words and seem to be lost? This is a very difficult place to be. I'm talking about personal pains that no one knows about, pains that have walked with you and slept with you. Perhaps some real pains are causing you to live on your knees like Hannah. You should take heart in the midst of this discomfort, because whatever leads you to your knees is worthwhile.

As Hannah's brokenness reached the ears of God, He gave her the desire of her heart. He had broken her for a reason. Due to her brokenness and need for a child, Hannah dedicated her only son, Samuel, to God, and among the Jewish prophets, Samuel was a special one.

When we see someone, we will never see a big sign on their foreheads that reads "Broken! I Have Fallen Apart!" On the contrary, broken people most often wear the most beautiful smiles. They only drop those smiles when they're in their closets bawling to God.

At times, people have made remarks about me, like "He's always smiling. He's a very happy guy." What they don't see is that hidden behind the smile on my lips, my heart has a bitter stench. Behind the blinds of my smile remain trails of sadness from a broken way. I can say, however, that my brokenness has given me the strong desire to help other broken people I see around me.

> If God has allowed you to be broken, it means that He is up to something.

As you are broken, be empowered to go on. Remember that God knows about your struggle, and He will come to rescue you. You must also remember that brokenness comes with purpose. If God has allowed you to be broken, it means that He is up to something. In your brokenness, be faithful like Hannah and continue to make your petition to God. God will come through at the right time, because His will must be done.

BROKEN PEOPLE HURT PEOPLE

There is a saying that tells us, "Hurting people hurt people." I find this to be very true. Most times, people who are deeply hurting do hurt others. In the pit of despair, our emotions are often all over the place. Unstable emotions will cause us to do things we wish we could undo. Maybe it's an angry father who never had a father of his own, and that's why he's doing such a bad job at fatherhood. Or maybe it's a young woman who's so damaged by past relationships that she decides to cut herself. It really doesn't matter what caused the hurt and the brokenness. We often allow our broken pasts to lead us toward a broken future.

This should never be so. If you are broken today, I understand you. I understand the emotions at play. I also understand that sometimes you do things without giving it a second thought. In no way am I saying that it's justifiable to hurt other people. All I'm saying is that I understand. My understanding is based solely on the fact that I've been there. I've been to a point where I was hurting the people around me because of my own deeply embedded hurts. I didn't understand how much harm I was causing until it was already done. In my mind I wanted to love, but all my actions accomplished were to hurt the people I was meant to love.

As a people, we are diverse, and so are the many things that break us. It's important for us to understand the vulnerable state we're in when we are broken. We should also be cognizant of the reality that it's very easy to hurt others when we ourselves are hurt. We should consider this and be careful in our dealings with the people we love, because words we speak can never be unspoken. The things we do can never be undone.

I believe that the grace of God can empower us to do all things. As we rely on His grace, we are able to overcome any hurt and brokenness. When your hurt burns, let it burn. The purpose of it is not to break you but to heal you.

BROKEN PEOPLE ARE OFTEN MISUNDERSTOOD

People are often very judgemental toward people who are hurting, without even trying to identify with their distress. It's easy from the outside looking in to assume what you would do if you were in the same situation. It's also nonsensical to think you can do better when you've never been in the same position. If you haven't taken each step of the broken, and felt every pain, you're not in a position to judge. If you haven't spoken their language and felt all their aches, you're not qualified to come to any conclusions about them. They need more help and less judgement. The Bible constantly admonishes us to cease from judging others. Paul the apostle asked the question: "*Who are you to judge someone else's servant? To their own master, servants stand or fall. And they will stand, for the Lord is able to make them stand*" (Romans 14:4). We aren't qualified to judge others. We need to see the sin but leave the sinner to his or her Maker, who is God. To God we stand, and to God we fall. People are people. Most often when faced with the same situations, we'll experience similar emotions, so we should be gracious and encourage the people around us.

Think of the Samaritan woman at the well long ago and how people judged her. As she fetched water from the well, Jesus approached her and began speaking to her. When the critics saw, they pointed out that Jesus was talking to a Gentile, but while they passed their judgements, the woman was receiving the water of life. Perhaps there's something to learn here, because often while the naysayers are busy talking, the broken are at the fountain, praying and filling their cups.

BROKEN PEOPLE NEED TIME TO HEAL

Time is the saviour of the broken, as given time and effort, our brokenness can be healed. There is an old saying that says, "Time heals all wounds." Brokenness is one of these wounds. Time will rid our brokenness as we seek to be healed. Brokenness requires time, faith, and divine love to heal.

Time is the gap between the temporal and the eternal, while faith is the vehicle to a place called love. In other words, time is the currency outside of eternity that causes things to happen. With time, things change, and change for the broken can be beautiful. The broken must be patient, because it takes time to undo years of hurt and pain.

For many of us, brokenness might be all we've known. In my earliest years, brokenness was a very good friend. Growing up, I always struggled because I thought I looked different than my peers. The truth is, no two people are fully identical, but Satan attacks us when we lack understanding. I was born with a slight injury to my left eye, and as a child I didn't know how to accept this difference. The worst thing for a child is feeling different. That's where my brokenness started, at a tender age, with other little children.

In school I was often teased. What could I have done as a child but be broken? My parents didn't understand because they didn't know, and as my peers were having fun, I was being torn apart. As a child who lacked understanding, I didn't know how to tend to my wounds when they bled. Now the question is: Can a few hours, a day, or even a year undo so many years of brokenness?

In my situation, and for most of us, the answer is no! I travelled with a hole in my heart for many years. I had needs that no one identified with. On one occasion as a teenager, I wanted to commit suicide, but my love for my family stopped me, as I didn't want to hurt them. The thought of my parents and siblings crying prevented me from committing such an act. As I grew older, I realized that God was with me all the time and that His grace had kept me in those times. His grace is sufficient for you regardless of your brokenness.

This is a brief synopsis of where I've been, but what about the little girl who was robbed of her innocence? What about the wife who is mercilessly beaten by her hurting husband, or is haunted by the memory of a stillborn child? I can't begin to understand the many pains, but I do know that given time, faith, and love, our brokenness can be changed into a blessing. As I write, I am not the most confident, and I haven't fully reached perfection, but I know that from a broken yesterday, I can be a blessing today. I write from a place of understanding because I know what it is to be broken.

As time passed, I began to understand who I was. This was mainly because I began to understand my true identity in Jesus Christ. I realized that I was fearfully and wonderfully made, and that I was just as valid and loved as anyone else. I began to experience and enjoy the true "me" God had created.

I want you to know that no amount of brokenness can take away your identity, and as you endure by faith, God will heal you by His grace. Be patient with your pain, because as sure as the sun rises, God will paint your pain away.

PAINT YOUR PAIN AWAY
He can paint your pain away,
And erase your stain away!
And sap your rain away,
Christ can crane your chain away!

Love can colour the clouded heart,
And fill the convoluted with art!
And trace your vain away,
Love can carry you in the day!

His light can spark the dark away,
And mark a way when there's no day!
Come what may, just if you stay,
He can reach you where you lay!

Oh, won't you faith your fear away,
And believe in His marvelous ray!
Don't succumb to the injury along the way,
For one day, Christ will paint your pain away!

BROKEN PEOPLE CAN DO BAD STUFF

I believe that many of the world's problems are caused by broken people. Some people are naturally evil, but others want to do good in the presence of evil. One day I was counselling a young man who had gotten himself in trouble with the law. I wanted to understand why he chose that path, so I asked him, "Why are you doing all this and hurting your family?" His response was that after a while, it became a habit and was hard to stop. As I spoke to him, I heard his contrition, yet he continued to do bad stuff.

I found out that he was from a broken family and had little to no relationship with his father. This young man was very broken, and the path he chose was breaking people. In my own life, I've hurt some people I love. I didn't want to hurt them, but due to my own hurt, I did. Brokenness can cause us to do things without thinking long enough, and often those things are bad. But brokenness is no excuse to hurt others. We shouldn't forget our responsibility to love others, even when we are broken.

Don't let your brokenness turn you into a monster. You are not a monster but a child of God. Satan wants to leverage your brokenness and cause you to carry out his evil intentions, but God wants to heal and transform you through your brokenness.

As you go, as you row, and as you cut through the waves of life, be encouraged through every broken place. Know that as sure as the sun rises to its summit, God in His great wisdom will work all things out for your good. I encourage you to love the Lord and do good.

JUDGE LESS AND LOVE MORE

It's easy to judge another person when they've done something we perceive as being wrong. However, perception is opinion, so we should seek the truth. We should never ignore the sins around us; instead, we should free the sinner from our judgements. Only God knows the complexities that haunt us, for He sees beneath the skin of our deepest tears. We see the debris that has covered up the real person, but God sees beneath the debris into the soul of that individual.

We should give one another the benefit of the doubt by judging less and loving more. The Apostle Paul asks the question: Why judge the next man's servant? We can't even begin to understand our own lives, yet we attempt to judge others. We're all in this together, and we all fall short at times. Jesus says that we must first take out the obstacle from our own eyes before we begin to judge others. The truth is, when we judge others, we open ourselves to the judgement of God. But if we love and forgive one another, we open the blessings of God over us. Jesus Christ, in His own words, gave us this teaching from the book of Matthew:

> *Do not judge, or you too will be judged. For in the same way you judge others, you will be judged, and with the measure you use, it will be measured to you. Why do you look at the speck of sawdust in your brother's eye and pay no attention to the plank in your own eye? How can you say to your brother, "Let me take the speck out of your eye," when all the time there is a plank in your own eye? You hypocrite, first take the plank out of your own eye, and then you will see clearly to remove the speck from your brother's eye.* (Matthew 7:1–5)

SEE BEYOND THE ACTIONS OF THE BROKEN

David was an adulterer, a murderer, and a cheater, but he was a man of God. God didn't define David by the bad stuff he did. He saw David in light of his heart. David's repentant spirit gave him the title of "*a man after* [God's] *own heart*" (1 Samuel 13:14). How can a man after God's own heart do such bad stuff? The reality is that sin exists, and we live in an imperfect world. When the rain falls, it falls for the just person and the unjust. This shows God's care for everyone, and we should be like God. Let's look beyond the faults of others and see them like God does.

We should never ignore the actions of a person when they pose a risk to us, but we should leave their judgement to the

Lord. In the end, God is a just judge, and He balances the books. Sometimes broken people pose a risk to us, especially when it comes to any form of violence. A person may be the victim of abuse and must seek safety. I believe God knows how to deal with the broken, and we should allow Him to do this. If you are broken, you should identify your need for help and seek assistance. Two broken people may have the passionate heart to help each other, but usually they can't. It is the intervention of the whole that will help the broken. As you are broken, seek the help of qualified people. Trust God that as you go, He will lead you beside still waters.

BROKEN PEOPLE YEARN FOR HEALING

I remember the times when I was overwhelmed with grief. At one point in my life, I looked back, and all I saw was a very broken road. At that point there were incessant tears as I pondered that road. I was fed up of being broken and I longed to be healed. When we've been in the fiery furnace of a broken place, we know how much the broken one desires healing. A broken place is a very hurtful place. When we understand the cry of the broken and their needs, we will be able to help them up. We will know that the broken genuinely yearn for help, even when they don't show it.

Be patient with the broken and hear what they have to say. Listen between the lines and hear the despair they enunciate. Broken people have very deep eyes—eyes so deep they house a well. Their countenance craves salvation, for the broken must be healed.

I once heard my cousin (who is a preacher) commenting on a drunkard he'd met at a church service. He was praying for this man, and as he prayed against the drunken spirit, the man cried out, "He is in there; he is in there. Come out of me; come out of me." This man craved to be free. He identified with his pain and wanted to escape, yet he couldn't. For him, this was a sign of freedom, and he cried out. This was the opportune moment for this man to be free!

On a cold winter day back in Canada, I was parked in a large parking lot and was bewildered with the grief of life. I remember I was playing the song "My Help Cometh from the Lord." As I listened to this song, I sensed the passing of freedom. I felt as if I could have been free, and I longed to be free. Instantly I bawled and bawled, because the more I poured out my spirit, the more I sensed my freedom. I didn't know I had the capacity to bawl with such power, but there I was, bawling out my soul. This was the cry of a broken soul. This was also the cry of a soul that yearned to be healed and felt as if healing was possible. Maybe you can identify with me. The broken one yearns for healing as the land yearns for rain in a drought. The reality is that we all want to get rid of our pain.

GOD IS IN THE HEALING BUSINESS

The book of Psalms speak about God sending His Word to heal His people (Psalm 107:20). God is in the healing business. There is no brokenness that God cannot reach with His love. As we go about our days, let's remember that we're not alone. There is a healing haven where God is the physician. This in itself is our healing, because as we believe, we receive. Sometimes the pain we endure is our process of healing. Keep heading in the direction of faith, knowing that God guides your every step. Your healing is taking place, and you have to believe this. Your job at every given point is to trust in the Lord and rely on His faithfulness.

Our brokenness appeals to the healing hands of God. Let's walk our paths knowing that nothing happens out of season. When we walk with God, our brokenness is God's purpose. Walk with God. Be strong in the battle, because God is the commander in chief. Your healing might be taking a little time, but time is the currency that purchases your healing. Be patient as you go, knowing that as you walk with God, He will feed you on His faithfulness.

HEALING IS THE CHILDREN'S' BREAD

God specializes in feeding us with His healing grace. In Matthew 15:22–29, we read about a woman who appealed to the healing grace of our Lord. This woman was a Gentile, and Gentiles were like dogs to the Jews of those days. The healing was for the children (the Jews), and she was an outsider asking for the mercy of Christ. The Bible says that the woman was willing to take even the crumbs from the Master's table, because she knew that the amount wasn't important but that healing came from the power of the One Who gave. When Jesus perceived the faithfulness of this woman, His answer was

"Oh woman, great is your faith! Let it be to you as you desire" (Matthew 15:28, paraphrased).

Our faith is what heals us. Our lack of faith limits our healing because you must believe to receive. May we be faithful, and may we receive the healing of God. The bread that we seek is not carnal bread but the Kingdom of God. Dear broken one, in your brokenness, you are being healed. Do your part by believing in the power of the healing of God. As you believe, your healing will be sure.

BROKENNESS CAN BE SUICIDAL

Life is a beautiful gift from God. The beauty of this gift can be seen all around us, from the graceful creation to the marvelous people we often interact with. Life is also the breath of God. The Bible says that God breathed into man, and he became a living soul (Genesis 2:7). The presence of life glorified God with the highest praise. Along our broken roads, we often become so engulfed in sorrow that we forget about this beautiful gift, yet no amount of forgetfulness can take away the truth of life—it is the precious gift of God. In John 14:6, Jesus says, "*I am the way and the truth and the life.*"

Amidst this, we hear of people taking their lives every day. According to the World Health Organization, over 700,000 people commit suicide each year, which amounts to one person taking their life every forty seconds.[4] This is the saddest thing

---

[4] "Suicide Prevention," World Health Organization, accessed August 12, 2023, https://www.who.int/health-topics/suicide#tab=tab_1.

a loved one will ever have to face. It's one thing to lose a loved one from natural causes, but to lose them to suicide has to be the highest form of pain anyone can endure.

I believe that the leading cause (and perhaps the only one) of this sad reality is brokenness. I don't think many people fully understand the true complexity of brokenness. If you've ever been burnt by physical fire, then you'll understand the scorching effects of this pain. No one wants to stay in the burning furnace of a fiery place. Our first and perhaps only response to burning flame is to get out of it as quickly as possible. Consider the soul-burning effect of a broken place. To burn in the spirit is synonymous to burning in the flesh, with an even greater impact. It's usually easier to get away from an external flame than from the inner burning of the soul.

Satan knows this very well. In the vulnerability of a broken place, Satan wants to snatch our life away from us, and we just want to escape. His trick is to get us to a place where we believe that our only escape is to die. Don't be fooled by this devil. God wants to hide you under the feather of His wings. In the depths of the complexity of brokenness, the diabolic forces rage. These forces are present to take your life away. The Bible says that the enemy has come to kill, steal, and destroy (John 10:10). Yet in all of this, Christ our Saviour has come to give us life.

In your brokenness, understand the forces that you're up against and the vulnerable position you're in. Brokenness can open up the gates of hell in your life if you allow it. Brokenness can also summon the healing power of God. When we're broken, it's easy to hide away from reality, yet that's the last thing we should do. During these times, we should seek help by all means necessary. Don't be afraid to seek help when you need it. Remember, Satan, your enemy, wants to snatch your life away from you, and you must never allow this. Don't be tricked into believing that you can do it all alone. If this was so, fewer people would hurt themselves in their brokenness. Brokenness is a place of need, so I implore you to seek help.

EIGHT
MOVING ON

MOVING ON ISN'T EASY

IT'S NOT EASY to move beyond a broken yesterday, but in order to give the future a chance, we must press forward. For the broken, often our brokenness is all we've known. One day in my late twenties, I was staring in the mirror, and all I could see were the remains of a broken yesterday. At that point I realized how much I was marred by the past. The bad roads I'd travelled, the dungeons I'd escaped, and the heavy loads all left evident marks on my life. On the one hand, these scars reminded me of yesterday's pain, but on the other hand, I saw where these marks cultivated fields of gold. On the canvas of yesterday, I saw the many colours of tomorrow.

In moving on you should never quit. Leave the quitting to cowards, because you are no coward. You are the product and the plan of God, and God is able to turn every wound into something worthwhile. The song writer says that "there is not a broken vessel that God cannot mend."[5] The scripture also

---

[5] James Payne, "Broken Vessel," NameThatHymn.com, accessed August 31, 2023, https://namethathymn.com/hymn-lyrics/viewtopic.php?t=277&start=20

says that God wants to give us beauty for ashes, and the oil of gladness for our mourning (Isaiah 61:3). Trust God. He wants to give us an abundant life, filled with purpose and truth.

> God is not our enemy. He is for us, and as we travel through our brokenness, He seeks to empower us with His healing grace.

God is not our enemy. He is for us, and as we travel through our brokenness, He seeks to empower us with His healing grace. You have what it takes to move from where you are into the kingdom of the perfect place of God. Your job is to keep pressing, to trust God, and to live. When you do this, it doesn't matter the number of trials and tribulations that come your way; God will bring you through every one of them.

> *"What shall we then say to these things? If God be for us, who can be against us?"* (Romans 8:31, ESV).

UNLOAD THE BURDEN

In order to be free, we must take hold of our freedom! As we do this, we must let go of the things that hold us back. It can be very complicated, because often we're so tightly affixed to the things that hold us back, it's hard to let them go. Sometimes we become so addicted to our own despair that we embrace it, but we must let go, because we must go on.

A wise person is one who does wise things, and I implore you to walk in the footsteps of the wise. It's not wise to travel with the scars of yesterday. The wise thing to do is to unload the burdens of yesterday in an effort to give tomorrow a chance. For many years I held to the agony of unforgiveness and hurt. I thought I was justified in remaining in my pain. I travelled with the hate, the resentment, and the hurt of a past I could never change. This wasn't good for me, and neither is it good for you.

Consider the children of Israel as they marched toward the promised land. At one point on their journey, they'd been going around Mount Seir for a long time. They couldn't advance to their divine destiny because they were living in the past. The Bible says that they longed to go back to the slavery of Egypt, yet God had prepared a better land for them. These were the same people who cried for freedom, and finally God had set them free. But they were so used to the brokenness of Egypt, they were afraid to walk into the promised land. We must let go of Egypt, and we must take hold of Holy Mount Zion. To do this, we must unload the burdens of yesterday and take hold of the beautiful reality of the future God has prepared for us.

There are over six billion people on the earth, yet you're the only one responsible for your future. God has given us the free gift of grace, which offers us fuel as we go. But we have to go. If you stay in the same place and do the same things, you'll always be the same—broken! It's said that the meaning of insanity is doing the same things over and over and expecting a different result. It just doesn't work that way. We must change our strategy to get a different result. We must move beyond the shattered dreams of yesterday and climb the hills of tomorrow.

When we do this, we will create for ourselves the promise of tomorrow. Remember, your future depends on your ability to unload the burden of yesterday.

REVIVE THOSE DREAMS

Brokenness at some point tends to want to steal our dreams from us. It makes sense that having gone through life's battering, we become distorted. Brokenness hurts, and hurt hinders. As we go and collect our pieces, let's revive our dreams and move on in faith. This is important, because some of our dreams are desires that God has placed within us to guide us to them. Dreams are like guides that keep us on track.

Growing up in the serene landscapes of the countryside, as an epitome of Eden, in those glorious corridors of lush greenery, I used to dream. As a child, absolved in the innocence of time, dreaming wasn't hard for me. I used to sit under heaven and wander into the expanse, and all that I saw was mine. Little did I know that there was a long gap, a great divide, between the playful, dreamy heart and the man I was to be. Given time and circumstances, some dreams began to fade—not because I didn't want them anymore, but reality started to unfold. Somewhere along the line, the dreams of wanting to buy a mini airplane to fly to school faded, and the dream of wanting to marry my childhood friend dispersed into the wind, because that's all they were—childhood dreams.

As I grew older, I started to experience what it was like to have a dream come true. I remember as explicitly as yesterday how I intensely yearned to attend the high school I eventually attended, and it was a dream come true. We're all dreamers, an ability endowed by the Creator of heaven and earth. We all had dreams, have dreams, and will continue to dream. Some dreams are so personal that they never die. Some are such that the power of their purpose won't permit them to lose courage. I believe that given the capacity to dream, God exercised the avenue to get us to the place where He wants us to go.

Joseph dreamt that his brothers would serve him, and though the Bible doesn't tell whether he believed in the dream, God knew what He was about. Joseph endured the test of time; he crossed the great divide that separated him from his dreams, and God the Master architect brought him there.

Oh reader, won't you believe in your dreams again? God won't permit your dreams to die, and neither should you. You must protect them, nourish them, and actively work toward achieving them. You should walk with the knowledge that God is for you and that He supports you in everything you do, even in your dreams.

HOPE IN THE LORD

Not everyone will make it through their brokenness. Some people give up along the way, while others stay the course. It's not by our own might but through the Spirit and the grace of our God that we overcome. The scripture says, "*Even youths grow tired and weary, and young men stumble and fall; but those who hope in the Lord will renew their strength*" (Isaiah 40:30–31). The Word "but" cancels all that comes before it.

The weariness, the brokenness, the tiredness—these are all cancelled when we hope in the Lord. There are two things that we have to understand here: who God is and who we are. God sits enthroned above the circle of the earth, never growing weary. We are fallible people with horrible hurts, where sin has left us wanting. When we realize who we are, we'll identify our need for a Saviour. When we come into revelation of who God is, we find that He is the Saviour we need. Hope in the Lord, because hope does not disappoint. As you hope, may the Lord relieve you of your brokenness!

HOPE DOES NOT DISAPPOINT

In Romans 5:3–5, Paul speaks of the great security we have when we hope in God. The verse says that tribulation brings about character, character hope, and hope does not disappoint. The victory we find when we hope is in the subject of our hope. In Jeremiah 29:11, the Lord says to His people, "*For I know the plans I have for you … plans to prosper you and not to harm you, plans to give you hope and a future.*" Imagine hoping in a God whose plan is to give you hope. This hope can never fail. In our short-sightedness, we might see otherwise. It might seem as if all hope is lost and that God isn't faithful concerning His Word. It is therefore important for us to see through eyes of faith and look beyond the present into the eternal hope God is giving us.

As we hope in God, He removes the blinds, and we can see behind the curtains of the present into the expanse of hope that awaits us. I haven't walked your path, so I might not fully understand you, but I know that they who wait upon the

Lord shall renew their strength. I also might not know the overwhelming complexities of the struggles you face, but I know that the Lord is merciful and faithful to those who trust in Him. Be of good courage and hope in the Lord from you heart.

Inevitably you'll move beyond your brokenness. The complex state of the broken is so uncomfortable that pressing forward is a must. At the end of the day, people vary, and so do their decisions. The coward will quit and submit to failure, while the courageous will stand in the face of the challenge and fight. Moving on may not be the most comfortable or less painful, but it's the wise thing to do. As we walk the corridors of time, let's not forget that we have the power to create and adjust, the power to steer in faithfulness the wheel of our life. May you hope into tomorrow.

REAL WOUNDS
These are real wounds, they belittle me,
Real wounds that beyond which I cannot see.
They cut so deep and mar so long.
These are wounds that break the strong.

Real wounds, wounds that put you in a cell.
These are wounds that scar so well.
They pierce so deep and slice so broad.
These wounds they leave a lot of flawed.

Oh, wounds of mine, real wounds of mine,
Wounds that leave me ever crying.

Wounds of mine, yet Jah shall hear.
He helps me up in my despair.

He heals the wounded one.
He strengthens the broken through His Son.
And in real wounds, as in wounds of mine,
The Lord will rescue every time!

IT WILL BE OKAY

As people of God, we must believe that all things will work together for good. Some people believe that the religious are the people of God, but we're all the people of God. The Bible says that He made all things through the power of His Word. We all fall under the umbrella of "all things." Paul writes in Romans 8:28: "*And we know that in all things God works for the good of those who love him, who have been called according to his purpose.*" As we keep our end of the bargain to love, we will see all the things that want to break us, make us.

As Jesus was led to the cross in an utterly broken state, He carried the weight of sin and also the weight of that rugged cross. In the natural, it seemed as if Jesus had lost the battle, but in the Spirit, He had conquered sin. They spat in His face and ridiculed Him, yet God used this brokenness to offer us resurrection life. As we die daily from the circumstances around us, let us hold tight to the fact that God has it all together. There is good news for the broken, for it will be okay. You deserve to be healed, and you will be healed as you believe it. All the trials and tribulations you go through will turn into something good when you believe and follow God.

The most tragic things that have happened in my life have caused some of the greatest good. In my destitution, I learn how to be patient; in my pain, I learn devotion. As I write, I write because I have been there and done that. I totally understand what it is to be broken, and that's why I'm writing to tell you that it will be okay as you trust in the Lord.

LITTLE BY LITTLE

We are healed little by little. Always remember that your pieces will take some time to be put back together. It takes courage to be strong, but find this courage and be strong. You have to be strong in the midst of the pressure, and you have to endure the little to embrace the big. Through little moments of healing, we achieve a life that is whole. It's a divine principle that things take a little time. Whether it be wealth, health, or healing, given time, things change, little by little.

We must identify with the little changes we make in the right direction. In these changes, we are healed. This is true in the natural as much as in the spirit. It is normal for things to happen bit by bit. God could have made the world in a second, yet it took Him six days. In this, God teaches us the principle that we must use to achieve almost everything we set out to achieve. Take heart—you are being healed in the back room, God's room. God is the one in the background of our lives connecting points and balancing the books. God wants to heal us little by little, over time. May we open our hearts and be healed as we go, little by little!

LEVERAGE YOUR BROKENNESS

A marriage that has been healed can become a pinnacle upon which other marriages find hope. A broken individual can be a saviour to those in need. As we are broken, let's use our brokenness to bless others. It's normal to be broken, but it's not normal to stay broken. Some people write songs about how they endured their brokenness, and these songs inspire millions to also endure. Some people write inspirational poetry, some people use their brokenness as a tool for counselling, and the list goes on. The key is to use your brokenness as a blessing, and then and there it will all make sense.

We receive a special anointing from our brokenness that can be a light in someone's darkness. Let's remember Who is walking with us as we go. God promises to be with us, and if God is with us, then it will all make sense. Take the eaglet, for example. While it's still in its shell, the mama eagle has to hover over the brood to create an intense heat source for the eaglet to hatch. This might be a very uncomfortable and undesirable time for the eaglet, but this is just the wisdom of God making new life. As we are broken, something great is happening to us. Embrace your brokenness and be strong.

In the dark brood of our brokenness, we will feel the heat and the discomfort, but God is up to something good. Let's look for the hidden lessons we must learn, and let's be empowered to empower. Life is a community, and in this community, we all empower each other in some way. I encourage you to change your perspective on brokenness, because in the dungeons of a broken place, God is at work.

NINE
THE BEST IS YET TO COME

EXPECT TO SEE THE GOODNESS OF GOD

WE MUST EXPECT the best in order to experience it. When we expect something to happen to us, we have faith that it will actually come to pass. This means that we must have no negative expectations for our lives. We must constantly believe that we will live to see the goodness of God in our situation. It might not seem at all possible, but we must be like David the psalmist, who said, "*I would have lost heart, unless I had believed that I would see the goodness of the Lord in the land of the living*" (Psalm 27:13, NKJV).

David was no doubt going through a hard time, as he said, "*I would have lost heart.*" It's in the most difficult of circumstances that we succumb to life's injuries. Yet in these same moments we can win life's greatest victories. It all has to do with how we view the situation and what we expect to happen to us. What if the psalmist didn't expect something good to happen? Do you believe he would have maintained his composure in the spirit? He gave us the answer when he said, "*I would have lost heart.*" The psalmist knew that because he held on to the fact that someday he would see God come through for him, he would make it in the end.

In the case of Job, his expectation was that after he had been tried by the fire of God, he would be refined into choice gold (Job 23:10). As Job searched for God in his situation, the scripture explains that though he couldn't see Him, he remained faithful. Job, like David, knew the power of positive expectations.

Now it's your turn. From this point forward, never again have a negative expectation for your life. Always expect and believe that though you might be going through your brokenness, when you have been fully tried, something good will happen.

GOD WANTS TO GIVE YOU A GREAT FUTURE

If you allow it, brokenness can bring you to a place of toxic hopelessness. The Bible assures us that God wants to give us a future and a hope. It might not seem like it, but the ultimate goal of God is to make our lives better. All the situations we experience are just agents of God, precisely positioned to bring us closer to where He wants us to be. This is a hard saying, especially for people who have experienced the ultimate trials of life, yet the wisdom of God can carefully manoeuvre us to safety. It's not what it appears to be, but it is what it really is. In other words, the truth is not in how we interpret what we don't understand, but the truth is what it is—the truth.

"For I know the thoughts that I think toward you, says the Lord, thoughts of peace and not of evil, to give you a future and a hope" (Jeremiah 29:11, NKJV).

The ultimate truth is that God wants to give us a future and a hope. Consider God, our good Father! Would a good Father want anything less for His child? Even evil men have good plans for their children, so consider then the great hope God wants to give the ones who depend upon Him. A good father will do what is necessary to give his children true hope.

Imagine that in order to give us eternal life, God had to sacrifice His only Son. Consider also that as Jesus marched to the cross, He could have stopped His own crucifixion, yet He was obedient to the point of death. The road to hope is often broken. Nonetheless, broken roads often lead to a beautiful destination. Because of the broken road Jesus chose, He gave us the chance to enter into the hopeful land of the Kingdom of God.

Life might not always seem hopeful, especially as we walk through the valley of the shadow of death, but remember that the road to eternity travels through death. In our great struggle, let's look beyond this world and into the expanse of our heavenly residence.

Don't be discouraged! God has gone before us, and He is constantly paving our way. When we know this, we will seek to endure our difficulty, because we'll know that our difficulty will lead us to a beautiful place. Continue to press! The Bible says that hope does not disappoint. It doesn't matter how hard life gets, it cannot take away the sovereign Word of God, which has promised us a future and a hope.

LOOK THROUGH EYES OF FAITH

The Bible says that without faith, it is impossible to please God (Hebrews 11:16), and that faith is the substance of the things we hope for, and the evidence of the things we do not see (Hebrew 11:1). Consider how important it is to be faithful as we travel along our broken roads. We can't have faith for the things we see and have but rather for the things we don't have. In our difficult time, we mainly have brokenness, so it gives us the perfect opportunity to hope for the thing we don't see, which is the wholesomeness of God in our situation.

Our hard times are just opportunities for us to have faith and to prove the power of God in our lives. It's also the time to activate miracles over our lives. We do this by looking through eyes of faith. When we look away from what we see and upon the things we don't see, we basically call the unseen into the seen. It is by our faith that we create our reality.

In our brokenness, we must envision the wholesomeness that God wants to bring us into. By doing this, we will begin to trust God to bring us to this place. We can't let our current situation determine the outcome of our lives. On the contrary, we must allow our faith to establish us. Let's see the things that are not present, so as to draw them closer to us. Let's trust the hands of the God we can't see, that He will work things out for us, and that ultimately He will enable us to see better days.

GOD IS FOR YOU, NOT AGAINST YOU

Through our brokenness, God is for us and not against us. He has good plans for our lives simply because He is for us. We might not be able to see it, but in all that we go through, the ultimate aim of God is to give us the best future we could ever hope for.

Solomon asked the question: *"For who knows what is good for man in life, all the days of his vain life which he passes like a shadow? Who can tell a man what will happen after him under the sun?"* (Ecclesiastes 6:12, NKJV). The answer to this question is God. God knows what is good for us in this life. When God prunes us, He gets rid of the unnecessary pieces of our lives to give us what He sees as meaningful and necessary. In these times, we should trust the sovereign hands of God. God doesn't want to break us permanently; He wants to establish us on a firmer foundation.

Among the many benefits of a hurricane/storm is that it gets rid of old and dead vegetation in order for new ones to grow. Growing up in Jamaica, we used to have many storms. Up to this day, I can remember their terrible impact. In the midst of a storm, it seems like everything is falling apart. The ruffling roofs and flying trees cause us to fear for our lives. Yet what I remember mostly is the calm after the storm. Many weak roofs blow off during storms, and weak roots will also give way. But after a storm, we see new roofs and new roots. The storm will get rid of the weak in order to make way for something stronger to be established.

Consider God as He works out our situations for His own good pleasure. In His sovereign wisdom, He knows exactly what He's doing. He knows the unnecessary pieces that only life's storms can get rid of. In my own journey, the most difficult storms have instilled the most love and compassion in my heart. Because of the wounds that caused me to bleed, I can have compassion on others who bleed. Similarly, some of the most heavenly-hearted people I know are the ones who have endured the roughest storms and survived.

I pray you'll be strong as you travel through your owns storms, and that you'll never succumb to the injury they will impose upon you. Have faith in the after-storm, that every little thing will be all right. Always remember that the best is yet to come.

TEN

LOVE NEVER FAILS

GOD IS LOVE

WHEN I SAY love never fails, what I'm really saying is that God never fails. The Bible says that God is love. The term used for the love of God toward us is *agape*, which denotes the most sacrificial and healing love. It is the love that would die on a cross to save all of humanity. When we understand this, we'll learn to trust God as we walk with Him. We will recognize that God, who is love, and who walks with us, will lead us beside still waters.

In our brokenness, it's important to recognize the finger-prints of God. I have a friend who always sings the song "He Was There All the Time!" As we pass through the valley of the shadow of death, God is ever present, and as long as He is with us, we will be okay. The severity of our brokenness doesn't matter; in fact, the more broken we are, the more we'll experience the miracle of God. In the book of 1 Corinthians, we read the most pure definition of love.

Love is patient, love is kind. It does not envy, it does not boast, it is not proud. It does not dishonor others, it is not self-seeking, it is not easily angered, it keeps no record of wrongs. Love does not delight in evil but rejoices with the truth. It always protects, always trusts, always hopes, always perseveres. Love never fails. (1 Corinthians 13:4–8a)

As we are broken, we should remember that God, Who is love, is with us. When God is with us, we can look forward to brighter days and see His glory in our lives. It doesn't matter the dark road we walk; let us seek to experience His resurrection, which will lift us up from our broken place.

IN THE DARK
In the darkness of the dark
Often souls find spark …
In the grave, in solitude,
Something cradles in the brood.

And often depths derail,
Sightlessness can hinder sail.
Yet dark awakes a light,
It's what happens after night …

For life is roused a deep,
Our flames find franchise as we sleep!
And lest a seed be gone away,
A seed's not rescued in the day!

Still faith finds courage when it's tested,
Death finds power resurrected.
Nothing can't hold me down.
If I die, I must rebound!

And at the darkest side of dark,
In Christ my soul shall spark.
For I find cradle in the deep …
And in my spirit, I'll ever leap!!

LOVE IS ALWAYS THE BEST ANSWER

We can fight fire with fire, which will bring more fire, or we can fight fire with water, which will calm our fires. Love, like water, will always calm our fires. In our brokenness, it often seems like we've been submerged in a fiery furnace, yet if we apply love in all situations, our brokenness will result in something more beautiful than what we started out with. The Bible says that love never fails, and it doesn't matter the great tribulations we might be walking through. When we love in truth, we can never fail.

The most natural response toward someone who has done us wrong is to want to repay them for what they've done. When someone steals something from us, our one aim is to get it back. Yet, as I stated earlier, we can't fight fire with fire. It's just not a wise thing to do. It's not about how we would naturally respond, or how we feel we should respond, but what God requires of us. The amazing truth about the requirement of God is that it's always the best option.

I know how hard it is to love someone who has done us wrong. This is especially hard when that person is close to us and continues to hurt our bleeding wounds. Yet no amount of fighting and hating can ever resolve our brokenness. Perhaps we're not healing because we're not loving. Love is a spiritual response, and it often doesn't make much sense in the natural. Yet when we truly love, we can never fail. Love is our weapon in the spirit that enables us to win.

On the opposite side of love is hate. This means that if we don't choose love, then we'll hate by default. As children of God, we should be aware of this, and we should deliberately seek to love one another, regardless of what they've done to us or how bad it feels.

Remember, it's not about how we feel but about what is right and best. There's no better way for us to overcome our brokenness than to love immeasurably, as God requires of us. This might not be easy, and this is where dying to self comes in. We have to literally be changed from our old mindset in order to truly love. Don't be afraid when you love; always remember that God will enable you to do what He requires of you.

> There's no better way for us to overcome our brokenness than to love immeasurably, as God requires of us. This might not be easy, and this is where dying to self comes in.

DYING TO SELF

One thing is for sure—the brokenness we experience can purge us of our impurities. Of course, this is dependent on how we view the circumstances we go through. If we view our brokenness as good, and if we expect to see God's grace and favour through it, then this is exactly what will happen to us. On the other hand, if we view our brokenness as an agent that has come to destroy us, then this is what it will do. We should be like Joseph, who said, "*But as for you, you meant evil against me; but God meant it for good, in order to bring it about as it is this day, to save many people alive*" (Genesis 50:20, NKJV).

As we are broken away from our former impurities and imperfections of self, we are built into a more loving, caring, and spontaneously empathetic individual. The Bible says that God wants to transform us into a perfect man (like Jesus Christ), and for this to happen, we must die of self. We've all been born in sin and shaped in iniquity (Psalm 51:5). This means that in order for us to be transformed, we must let go of this old person. If we were perfect, we wouldn't be broken. Our brokenness attests to our imperfection and proves how much we need to let go of this imperfect person in order to take on the perfection God wants to bring us into.

> *You were taught, with regard to your former way of life, to put off your old self, which is being corrupted by its deceitful desires; to be made new in the attitude of your minds; and to put on the new self, created to be like God in true righteousness and holiness.* (Ephesians 4:22–24)

Here we see Paul encouraging us to die to the old self. It's quite evident that there's an old man that is not good for us. In our brokenness, God is helping us to get rid of this old man, and as hard as it might feel at times, He literally has to break us away from this person, hence we experience our brokenness. We can safely conclude that our brokenness didn't come to destroy us, though we may be hurting, but to give us new life in Christ. Unless a seed dies in the ground and sheds its old skin, it will never grow into the newness of life it was created for. Our spirits must be stripped of all unrighteousness, filthiness, and folly, and we must be transformed into the holiness and perfection of our Great High Priest.

HURTING CAN BE HEALING

There's a difference between harm and hurt. Often our lack of understanding affects how we view the Word of God. Even though an activity, such as an exercise, may hurt you temporarily, it doesn't necessarily mean that the body is being harmed. Sometimes hurt is just a sign that harm is coming. On the other hand, when someone deliberately inflicts a wound on you with an evil intention, they seek to harm you.

Hurt often isn't intentional but just a sign that change and adjustment are needed, whereas harm is deliberate, and the intention behind harm is evil. Consider God as a good Father dealing with His children. He might hurt us for a while in order to prevent us from being harmed. This means that if God sees us going down the wrong way, He might put up a roadblock that will cause us to fall down and get bruised. The real harm to be done here isn't by God stopping you but by you going down the road He has blocked.

Often our brokenness isn't meant to harm us but to prevent us from getting truly harmed. The true harm to the human being is to be spiritually cast into hell, and sometimes God has to literally hurt us in order to prevent us from the true harm of eternal damnation. When we understand this, we will endure our brokenness from a place of understanding, knowing that though we might be struck down, we will not be destroyed. The Apostle Paul said it this way: "*We are hard pressed on every side, but not crushed; perplexed, but not in despair; persecuted, but not abandoned; struck down, but not destroyed*" (2 Corinthians 4:8–9, NKJV).

Paul knew that even though he was being torn apart in the flesh, in the spirit he was being renewed and transformed. The true injury of life isn't being struck down but rather being destroyed. As we experience the brokenness of life, we should remember that our brokenness didn't come to harm us but to inevitably bring us into the Kingdom of God and His healing.

The problem is not in the promise of God but in the way we understand His promises. God's goal is to transform us into the stature and measure of the fulness of Christ, and He will do just this. Sometimes God will stir up our nests in order to teach us how to fly. It might also mean that He will have to chasten us, as the scriptures say: "*For whom the Lord loves He corrects, just as a father the son in whom he delights*" (Proverbs 3:12, NKJV).

We should take God at His word, regardless of our limited sight and point of understanding. God is not a man that He should lie. He cannot make a mistake, and He cannot do wrong. When we understand this, we will live from a place of faith rather than fear. We will know that however hard our lives may seem, God is with us. When we go through the valley of the shadow of death, He is there, to the very end of our lives.

It doesn't matter what a situation seems like. Faith will tell us that it is not a feeling that justifies God's presence, but it is His Word. This means that it doesn't matter how we feel; what matters is what the Word of God says. Our lack of understanding doesn't take away from the true meaning of the Word of God.

ELEVEN

FAITHFULNESS IS YOUR BEST BET

FAITH IS MOST NECESSARY

BROKENNESS CAN CRIPPLE you. If you allow it, brokenness can also turn you into a monster. Don't ever allow this to happen. You have the power to steer your brokenness in a positive direction. Sometimes we don't choose the ways in which we have been broken, but we always have the power to choose how we respond to our brokenness. Be faithful as you're torn apart, because faithfulness is the best response to your brokenness. While we are faithful in our great distress, God will be faithful to His Word. The Bible says, "*If we are faithless, He remains faithful, for He cannot disown himself*" (2 Timothy 2:13). This means that even when we have been faithless in our depravity, God will still be faithful to who He is as a Redeemer, simply because He cannot deny who He is.

The most important thing in this life is to walk a good path of faith, which means following the Word of God and walking in love. As we are broken, our values will also be challenged. In this time, we must remain resolute to be better and not bitter, because if we don't deal with our brokenness faithfully, it will cause us to become and remain bitter.

In your brokenness, you must constantly believe that victory belongs to you because of whose you are. You are a child of the living and faithful God, and you have what it takes to gain victory over your circumstances. Be strong!

DON'T BECOME BITTER, BECOME BETTER

In your brokenness, it's important to know the forces you're up against. The Bible says that we don't fight against flesh and blood but against powers of darkness in high places. In our brokenness, there is the power of God, and then there is the force of darkness at work. On the one hand, God wants to make you better, and on the other hand, the forces of evil want to make you bitter and turn you into a monster. In these trying moments, be keen to guard your heart. The scripture says, *"Above all else, guard your heart, for everything you do flows from it"* (Proverbs 4:23).

Be careful of the thoughts you allow to flow through you as you travel through your pestilence. This is so important, because whatever you allow to get into your heart will rule your emotions and your life. It's true that as a man thinks in his heart, so he will be. To know this truth is to be fully prepared when you're called upon. In the midst of whatever you go through, remember that there are two forces at work. You must also know with all your heart that God is with you in your brokenness, and that given time in worship and faith, He will deliver you. You must also walk with the wisdom that there are enemies that want to destroy you. Your victory is to walk by faith with God. As you do this, God promises to make your enemies your footstool.

At times in my life I allowed brokenness to make me bitter and not better. At one point I was so bitter toward people who'd done me wrong that it caused me to respond to situations in ways I could never be proud of. As I remained bitter, I became more broken. My heart was so drenched with sorrow and hurt that it became clouded with the fog of despair.

The good news in all this is that it wasn't the end for me. During this time, I became bedridden with sorrow. For days I didn't get out of bed except to eat. I slept almost twenty-four hours every day for almost a week. During that time I tried to reach out to friends and family, but usually they were busy. All I was left with was bitterness and enclosed walls of grief. At that time, I realized that the pain of bitterness was too much for me. I also realized that bitterness only leads to more bitterness. I was responding to situations out of negative emotions rather than love. This I find to be most detrimental.

Afterwards, I had to change. When the pain of staying bitter became unbearable, I realized it would inevitably hurt me, as the burden of bitterness is a very heavy load to carry. I had to take on the yoke of Christ. The scripture says that His yoke is easy and His burden is light (Matthew 11:30). I started to pray and ask God for strength and guidance, and I also started to forgive the people who had done me wrong and to move on. This wasn't an easy process, and it happened little by little.

In this time, I tried to hold on to the small victories I made each day and not look at the big situation as a whole. While I did this, I started to experience the change of God. It didn't happen in one day, but each individual day I felt lighter and lighter as I started to do the right thing. It didn't mean that I suddenly became perfect, but I suddenly had a perfect heart toward getting things right.

At the end of the day, I learnt one very important lesson in this encounter: it is far more profitable and blessed to get better and not bitter in our brokenness. I also found that the one who is restored is the one who resolves to walk by faith with God.

EXPECT TO HAVE AN AMAZING FUTURE

Don't ever conclude that because you're broken, it's the end. It is not the end. In fact, as you walk with God, each day is a new beginning. Each day is a next perfect opportunity to renew your mind and continue your journey. Don't allow the circumstances you face to cause you to believe you can't recover and have an even more amazing life than before. In your brokenness, you should expect to see something good come out of your situation. David said it like this:

> *I would have lost heart, unless I had believed that I would see the goodness of the Lord in the land of the living. Wait on the Lord; be of good courage, and He shall strengthen your heart; wait, I say, on the Lord!* (Psalm 27:13–14, NKJV)

As you experience your brokenness, don't ever have a bad expectation for your life, as this is far too dangerous. An expectation is so powerful that it will often happen in front of your eyes. What you expect to happen is what you believe will happen. And what you believe you receive.

David's expectation was to live to see the glory of God in his living days. David was a great king, with great faith, possessions, and wisdom. God blessed David beyond measure because of what David expected to happen to him in his life. Are you able to do the same? Are you able to expect God's best no matter what?

When I look back at all the negative encounters I've had in my life, many of them were things I feared would happen. They were the things that ran through my mind on a regular basis. Eventually I saw them manifest in my life so clearly that I decided never to have a negative expectation again. I want to encourage you to do the same. It's not me but God who requires your positive expectations. God doesn't want you to expect to see anything but His glory and the manifestation of His power in your life.

You might be going through the roughest of times, but don't give up. You can expect and see God's goodness in your life. If you feel that you've done too much wrong and that you don't deserve to see better days, you are wrong. The Bible says that His grace is sufficient for you. You can do all things though Christ who is able to strengthen you, and getting over your brokenness is one of these things you can do. In all of this, expect that God will be gracious to you and that He will show you the way to escape your brokenness and reach a place that is whole.

> *"Not that we are sufficient of ourselves to think of anything as being from ourselves, but our sufficiency is from God"* (2 Corinthians 3:5).

TWELVE
DEALING WITH NEGATIVE EMOTIONS

ANGER, HURT, AND hate are just some of the negative emotions we experience when we're broken. It's important to understand these emotions and learn how to deal with them. We must realize that we are human, and humans become hurt while broken. Hurt, when not dealt with properly, will lead to anger and hate. When these two emotions aren't addressed, they open up the doors of evil in our lives. We must pay keen attention to these emotions and not allow them to find roots and grow in us.

We must first understand our vulnerability while we're broken. When a person is broken, they become so fluid that they can easily become better or bitter. Think about water's ability to take on the shape of its container. Brokenness will make us as fluid as water. While being broken, we become so selfless and in need of help that we usually fall victim to our source of help. In other words, we usually take on the shape of the environment from which we seek help. If a person goes to church to seek help, they usually become more church-like;

similarly, if a person seeks help from drugs and alcohol, they usually take on the character of these things.

In our brokenness, we must avoid anger and hurt and every other form of negative emotion at all cost. When we indulge in these negative emotions, we take on their form. A person who resorts to anger will become angrier. A person who continually becomes angry will open up the door to many other forms of sin. Similarly, when a person is hurt and continues to hurt, this can cause them to hate whatever or whoever has hurt him/her. On the other hand, if these emotions are dealt with in the proper way, they can lead a person into a changed life. If while we're angry we seek to let go of our anger by loving, and if when we're hurt we allow Jesus Christ to heal our brokenness, we will become a more loving, wholesome individual.

We must constantly remind ourselves that though we might be broken and hurt, God is able to turn our lives around. We must trust Him. As we do this, we will experience the life-changing effect of faith as He makes us whole!

THE BATTLE IN THE MIND

The mind is a battlefield. I once read a book called *Battlefield of the Mind*, and I must commend author Joyce Myers for such a great work. Indeed, the mind is a battlefield! This is not a battle that we choose; it's by default that there's a battle within us. Each day, thousands of thoughts run through our minds. These thoughts are influenced by the things we listen to, the things we see, and the people we associate with. They are also a motivating factor in the way we respond to life. In order to have an outward victory, we must first win this battle in our minds.

To win this battle, we must refill our minds with the attitude of a winner. The first step toward this is to know that there is a battle going on. We must then be educated on how to win this battle. The Bible says that we do not fight against flesh and blood (physical people) but against principalities and powers and spiritual forces of evil in the heavenly realms (Ephesians 6:12). In this verse we learn that our true enemy isn't one that we see and feel, but one who attacks us from within. Our true enemies are the thoughts that come to change our perspectives of who we are, and the philosophies that want to pervert our heavenly origins. These enemies can only attack us from the inside, so we should learn the saying "win from within!"

We must be keen to accept good thoughts into our hearts and shield out bad ones. Not every thought that goes through our minds truly represents us, but if we let these thoughts into our hearts, they will become a part of us. Solomon said it like this: "*as he thinks in his heart, so is he*" (Proverbs 23:7, NKJV). What you choose to do on the battlefield of your mind will determine whether you'll be a victor or be defeated. In the midst of our brokenness, what we really struggle with is a broken mind. If we can fix our broken minds, we can fix our broken lives and hearts.

In order to fix our broken minds, we must adapt a new mind. For the children of God, this new mind is the mind of Christ. Earlier I shared how I struggled with self-esteem issues in my early years, and how as I began to learn about who I was, I began to heal from this brokenness. As we adapt a new perspective, we will also adapt a new life. God wants to give us a new life, and the way He does this is by giving us a new mind. The Bible says that we have the mind of Christ: "*'For who has understood the mind of the Lord so as to instruct him?' But we have the mind of Christ*" (1 Corinthians 2:16). In our brokenness, we must take hold of this new mind in order to be healed.

FIRST DEAL WITH WHAT IS GOING ON

It's very important to deal with things in our lives in order to prevent them from turning into unrepairable, life-crippling situations. I can tell you from my own experience that it's better to deal with a small problem than with a big one. Not dealing with a smaller problem can lead to the destruction of lives, marriages, and communities.

The enemy knows this very well, so he often deceives us into believing that if we just leave things alone, they'll go away. This is not so. When you don't deal with the conflicts in your mind, they will continue to live with you and be a part of you. They build up negative emotions like anger, hate, and resentment within you. You must ensure that this doesn't happen in your life. The pain that can result from situations that get out of hand can be vast and devastating.

There is a Jamaican proverb that says "one one cocoa full basket." This proverb tells about the power of things adding up. When you fill a basket one by one (with anything), it will eventually be filled. This is the same when we allow little problems to fill our baskets over time. Imagine a basket full of problems! Be diligent to tend to your problems from early on. By doing this, you will close the doors of evil in your life, and you will welcome a future full of the light of God.

FIXING YOUR MIND WILL FIX YOUR LIFE

As I stated earlier, the mind is a battlefield. When you win on the battlefield of your mind, you win on the battlefield of your life. It's therefore important to deal with the mind in order to overcome your brokenness. You must train your mind with a wholesome and renewed mindset in order to achieve a wholesome and renewed life. As the scriptures say, "As a man thinks in his heart, so is he" (Proverbs 23:7, paraphrased). This means that if you think you are broken, then you are broken. On the other hand, if you think that you're whole, then you're whole. What we believe, we receive, so believe good things about your life and expect to experience those good things. As you do this, you'll begin to experience the wholeness you believe in, and to live the life God created you to live.

As we fix our minds, we should take note of what we're thinking and the thoughts that go through our minds. The scripture says it like this: "*We demolish arguments and every pretension that sets itself up against the knowledge of God, and we take captive every thought to make it obedient to Christ*" (2 Corinthians 10:5). This scripture states that we can think about what we're thinking, and when we're not thinking right, we can make our wrong thoughts obedient to the Word of God. In other words, we can refuse negative thoughts by dismissing them, and accept thoughts that are in line with the Word of

God. As we do this, we will begin to experience the change of God—first in our minds, then in our lives.

RECONSTRUCT YOUR MIND

As a man thinks in his heart, so is he. What we think is the greatest leader of our life. We may think the serene and the wonderful, or we may cogitate cynicism and lust. The mind must be reshuffled and rearranged if ever we should change. We need to adapt a new thought, and God calls this the mind of Christ—the mind of love that never fails and of peace that ever prevails.

This takes time, but time is the currency. With time and effort, we purchase the redemption of our lives. The broken one must realize that they have been marred with a broken mind, and this mind must be healed. This healing is a reconstruction of the whole landscape of the mind. It's a recourse and a shift in the attitude of the mind. For us to be relieved of our brokenness, we must first be relieved from a broken mind through reconstructing it.

Let's take a look at the mind of Christ. This is the mind of God, and the mind of God is God. As a result, we must put on God in the valley of our brokenness. Don't lose heart—all things are possible to him who believes. We must believe, because to believe is the breakthrough for the mind. Whatever we believe, we give life to, and life lives. The things we believe in our lives, live in our lives. If we believe in bad outcomes, then even a good outcome may seem bad, but if we believe in the good, then we will experience the goodness of life. Change your mind, change your life.

The Bible speaks about taking every thought captive to make them obedient to Christ. As we move along and walk our broken roads, let's be vigilant in protecting our minds. The mind is a battlefield, but we can win this battle with the right armour. We should put on peace, faith, and righteousness, because these are our weapons from God. Let us put on the armaments of the Spirit and shield our minds. We must undo what has been done. As we filter our thoughts, we must entertain newness to rid the old. We must read new books, listen to new material, watch new movies, etc. in order to cultivate a new mind.

Our minds must be refilled with a different mind. They must be filtered from all negativity, and our hearts must be drained of all despair. It's about moving from a place of brokenness to a place of wholeness. Be adamant and meticulous in the filtering of your mind, and be consistent when you try. If at first you don't succeed, try and try and try again.

One great activity you can practise in renewing your mind is meditating. By meditating I mean to ponder on the Word and the works of God. One of my favourite activities is to walk along the parks and meditate on the natural beauty of God. When I do this, I reflect on the Word of God and relate it to all I see around me. This activity helps me to remain positive throughout the day. As you go, and as you row, and as you cut through the waves of life, find some time and meditate, and in doing this, filter your mind to be in alignment with the mind of Christ.

TRAIN YOUR MIND

We must undo the bad habits of the mind. The mind often defaults to negativity, but we must shield out negative thoughts. Each time a negative thought comes, catch yourself and shield it away. When it comes again, shield it again. It's in this battle of shot and shield that our minds learn how to be new. The Bible is a great mind-changer. In the treasuries of the Word of God, there is the antidote to toxic thoughts. The Word of God is sharp, and it's quick and able to overthrow every negativity.

Consider the things you've been thinking. After careful consideration, take a look at your life and the direction in which you're going. Do your thoughts impact your life? If so, you should do something about this. Our thoughts can either make us bitter or better. As you go about your day, ensure that you are in charge of what you're thinking. Practise shielding negative thoughts and replacing them with positive ones. The mind is like a garden. If we plant good seeds, we get a good crop, but if we plant weed, we get weed. A broken mind will lead a broken life, but a life filled with the thought of God will produce a life of purpose and power.

I cannot say this enough: time is a currency that purchases our freedom. This means it will take time and effort to train your mind, but be patient in continuing. Remember, they that wait on the Lord shall renew their strength.

AS YOU CUT THROUGH THE WAVES OF LIFE

As you go, as you row,

and as you cut through the waves of life,

Don't let go when currents flow, the wind it whistles like a fife.

As you sow, you will grow, if you keep ploughing in the night,

And watering in the plight, for sure it will be all right.

There might be bellows in the deep and thunders in the steep,

Yet hold your forth while becoming, at the gate you keep.

And anchor your sail, for the sailors of God shall ever prevail,

And the wailers are the ones that have engaged the full tale.

Don't be fearful going north,

though the torrents may be raging,

And war may be waging,

know that you serve the Highest King,

And that He sees you, that He hears the song you render,

And that to His sound these same waves shall surrender.

Oh, you who press on, don't let the waves distract you,

For sure, God Most High will carry you through.

The waves of life, as you cut through these waves,

For sure, for sure, King Jesus saves!

BIBLIOGRAPHY

Goodreads. "Bob Marley Quotes." Accessed August 12, 2023. https://www.goodreads.com/quotes/884474-you-never-know-how-strong-you-are-until-being-strong.

Payne, James. "Broken Vessel." NameThatHymn.com. Accessed August 31, 2023. https://namethathymn.com/hymn-lyrics/viewtopic.php?t=277&start=20

Smith, Donald. "Sometimes It's Best to Burn Your Ships." ME&A. September 7, 2022. https://www.meandahq.com/sometimes-its-best-to-burn-your-ships/.

The Spurgeon Center. "The Cause and Cure of a Wounded Spirit." Accessed August 12, 2023. https://www.spurgeon.org/resource-library/sermons/the-cause-and-cure-of-a-wounded-spirit/#flipbook/.

World Health Organization. "Suicide Prevention." Accessed August 12, 2023 https://www.who.int/health-topics/suicide#tab=tab_1.

NOTES

www.ingramcontent.com/pod-product-compliance
Lightning Source LLC
Chambersburg PA
CBHW021932040426
42448CB00008B/1025